You Can Make a
Difference
Stories that touch the heart

Books and Booklets By J.P. Vaswani

In English:

101 Stories For You and Me
108 Pearls of Practical Wisdom
108 Simple Prayers of a Simple Man
108 Thoughts On Success
114 Thoughts on Love
A Child of God
A Day with Dadaji
A Mystic of Modern India
Begin the Day with God
Beloved Dadaji
Conversations with Dadaji
Dada Answers
Daily Appointment With God
Daily Inspiration
Doors of Heaven
Education: What India Needs
Feast of Love
Five Fragrant Flowers
From Darkness Into Light
From Hell to Heaven
Glimpses
Glimpses Into Great Lives
God In Quest of Man
Hinduism
How to Have Real Fun Out of Life and other Talks
How to Make Your Life A Love Story
How to Overcome Temptations
How to Overcome Tensions
I Have Need of You
I Luv U, God!
Invest in the Child
Joy Peace Pills
Laugh Your Way to Health
Life After Death
Life is A Love Story
Love and Laugh!
Nestle Now
Notes from the Master's Lute
Pictures and Parables
Positive Power of Thanksgiving
Prayers of a Pilgrim
Prophets and Patriots
Sadhu Vaswani: His Life and Teachings
Little Lamps
Secrets of Health and Happiness
Shanti Speaks
Snacks for the Soul
More Snacks for the Soul
Stories for Meditation
Stories for You and Me
Teach Me to Pray
Tear-Drops (poems)
Temple Flowers
Ten Commandments of A Successful Marriage
The Holy Man of Hyderabad
The Kingdom of Krishna
A Little Book of Life
A Little Book of Wisdom
The Little Book of Prayer
The Little Book of Service
The Little Book of Success
The Little Book of Yoga
The Little Book of Freedom From Stress
The Magic of Forgiveness
The Simple Way
The Story of a Simple Man
The Way of Abhyasa (How to Meditate)
Ticket to Heaven
Twinkle, Twinkle Tiny Star
What you would like to know about Karma
Whispers
Why Do Good People Suffer?
You Are Not Alone!
You Can Be a Smile Millionaire

In Hindi:

Alwar Santon Ki Mahaan Gaathaayein
Atmik Jalpaan
Atmik Poshan
Bhale Logon Ke Saath Bura Kyon
Chitra Darshan
Dainik Prerna
Krodh Ko Jalayen, Swayam Ko Nahi
Mahan Purush Jeevan Darshan
Santon Ki Lila

**Published by
Sterling Publishers Private Limited**

You Can Make a
Difference

Stories that touch the heart

J. P. Vaswani

Compiled by
Dr. Prabha Sampath
and
Krishna Kumari

A Sterling Paperback

STERLING PAPERBACKS
An imprint of
Sterling Publishers (P) Ltd.
A-59, Okhla Industrial Area, Phase II, New Delhi-110020
Ph.: 26387070, 26386165 Fax: 91-11-26383788
E-mail: ghai@nde.vsnl.net.in
www.sterlingpublishers.com

You Can Make a Difference: Stories that touch the heart
© 2006, J.P. Vaswani
ISBN 81 207 3153 0

All rights are reserved. No part of this publication may be reproduced, stored in a retrieval system or transmitted, in any form or by any means, mechanical, photocopying, recording or otherwise, without prior written permission of the publisher.

Published by Sterling Publishers Pvt. Ltd., New Delhi-110020.
Lasertypeset by Vikas Compographics, New Delhi-110020.
Printed at Sterling Publishers Pvt. Ltd., New Delhi-110020.

Contents

1. You Can Make a Difference!   9
2. As Long As God Is Awake ...   12
3. Throw Out Impure Thoughts   13
4. Kicking a Bad Habit   15
5. Where Are Their Mothers?   17
6. A Conqueror's Attitude   19
7. Annie Besant Learns About the Law of *Karma*   20
8. A Mirage   23
9. For the Love of My Brothers   24
10. The Wheel of *Karma*   27
11. Have We Forgotten Prayer?   32
12. Ticket to Heaven   34
13. For the Love of God   36
14. It Was a Silent Prayer!   39
15. Turn to God   40
16. Doing Away with Ego   42
17. The Value of *Satsang*   45

18.	Walking 'the Little Way'	50
19.	Avali's Wrath	52
20.	Ty Cobb's Batting Average	55
21.	The Best Kind of Prayer	57
22.	Doing Our Best	58
23.	Just a Minute!	60
24.	The Happy Peasant	61
25.	Compassion First	64
26.	Money Can't Buy Happiness	65
27.	Let the Mind Be Pure!	66
28.	The Prayer of Denial	69
29.	Be Like the Tiger, Not the Fox!	73
30.	The Suitor of Wales	75
31.	Are We Really Free?	76
32.	Only a Woodcutter	78
33.	A Friend Indeed!	81
34.	The Smell of Money	83
35.	I Offer Myself!	89
36.	Obeying Instructions	91
37.	The Spirit of Acceptance	92
38.	O Ye of Little Faith!	93
39.	The 'Man Eater'	95
40.	Let Nothing Block Your Horizon!	100

41.	Do You Like What You Are Doing?	101
42.	The Secret of Yoga	102
43.	Empty Hands	106
44.	Running Straight	108
45.	My Father is Holding the Rope	110
46.	Bald Before His Time!	111
47.	You Need a Ladder!	112
48.	Association With a Saint	115
49.	More than Human	117
50.	The *Baniya* and the Sepoy	119
51.	God Is!	126
52.	We Are Responsible for What Happens to Us	128
53.	Live and Let Live	131
54.	The Greatest Honour	133
55.	Not *Work!*	136
56.	Six Eggs for a Good Cause	138
57.	No Short Cuts	139
58.	Serve Silently!	141
59.	There's a Fine to be Paid	143
60.	He Cared for People	145
61.	Because I Love You …	146
62.	Is Not the Thief Your Brother?	147
63.	Persistence Pays!	149

64.	Leave It to God!	151
65.	Do Your Duty!	153
66.	The Answer to His Prayer	155
67.	The Influence of Television	156
68.	You've Got to *Give* to Get!	159
69.	Redefining Success	161
70.	Duty First	163
71.	Stone Soup	164
72.	Even God Changed His Mind!	168
73.	Sharing God's Blessings	171
74.	I Refuse to Be Negative!	173
75.	The Power of Kindness	175

You Can Make a Difference!

I read of a little girl called Isis Johnson. At the tender age of four, she took a gigantic step, which made a profound impression on her community.

At that time, the world was waking up to the horror of the dreadful condition of the people of Ethiopia. The country had been ravaged by a severe famine, and men, women and children were dying of malnutrition. Watching the heart-rending pictures of children like herself on television, little Isis said to her grandmother, "Can't we send the leftover food in our fridge to the children of Ethiopia?"

"No, my dear," said her grandmother. "Ethiopia is very far away, and the food will be spoilt by the time it gets there."

But Isis was not one to give up easily. "Aren't there any hungry children in our town?" she asked. "Surely we can share our food with them."

And so it all began. Little Isis went from door to door, asking her neighbours if they had some food to spare for hungry children. And thus began the Isis Johnson Foundation which distributes food and

clothes and other necessities to thousands of people all over the United States. Isis is a young lady of eighteen today. She hopes to become a doctor, so that she will be able to serve the ailing and the afflicted. Isis says, "It does not matter who you are; it does not matter if you are rich or poor. Everyone can make a difference. Everyone can help. All you have to do is to care!"

"There is not much that I can do on my own," is what many of us think. We are mistaken. The tragedy for many of us is not that our aim is too high and we miss it – but rather that our aim is too low and we reach it!

As Long As God Is Awake …

A mother and her child were alone at home one night. When they were about to get into bed, the mother switched off the light and the room became dark. A sudden fear gripped the child. The woman opened the window, and up in the sky, the moon shone bright.

"Mother, is the moon God's light?" asked the child.

"Yes dear," replied the mother.

"Will God switch off His light when He goes to sleep?" asked the child anxiously.

"No, my dear," said the mother. "God never goes to sleep, and His light is never switched off."

"Well then," smiled the child. "As long as God is awake, I'm not afraid!"

This is the reassurance that we can all have – our Father is always awake. Why should we give in to stress when His light shines upon us?

Throw Out Impure Thoughts

We are told that the Devil once called a meeting of all his associates. The forces of evil were all present at the meeting – each one boasting of his victories and conquests. Anger, envy, greed and jealousy were all boasting of their numerous victims. Soon a heated argument ensued: who, among them, could take the credit for wreaking the greatest havoc on mankind?

Impurity won, hands down. Conferring the dubious distinction upon him, the Devil himself remarked: "He is the one with the sharpest sword, the deadliest poison. All he has to do is to sow a single thought of impurity in the mind and it is enough to cause the greatest havoc."

I am reminded of my Beloved Master, Sadhu Vaswani. When he was a student, he carried a pin with him. Whenever an angry or negative thought entered his mind, he would prick himself with the pin, so that the impure thought could be thrown out at once.

Following his example, I too developed the habit of stopping every impure thought in its tracks. I would slap myself sharply, when an undesirable thought came to me.

"Was that a mosquito?" my friends would ask me. "Yes, the deadliest," I would reply. For truly, there is no mosquito worse than an undesirable thought!

Kicking a Bad Habit

There was a young man who had become a chain smoker at the age of 20. When he turned 21, he made a firm resolve to give up smoking for good.

"I have smoked hundreds of cigarettes," he said to himself. "Now it is time to give up this habit, which, I'm afraid, is turning into an addiction."

On the first morning after his resolve it was easy going for him. There was no urge to smoke. The morning passed quickly. But, when he sat down to lunch in the afternoon, he found that his meal was incomplete without a puff. He succumbed to the temptation and had a smoke. This was repeated day after day. Every morning he made a fresh resolve not to smoke but every afternoon he broke it.

Mark Twain, too, says: "Smoking is the easiest habit in the world to give up. I ought to know – I have given it up a thousand times!"

And so did this young man. But yet he did not give up and accept failure. Every day he reaffirmed to himself: I have not failed, but I have not yet succeeded. Surely there will come a time when I will give up smoking. His affirmation was one of latent though not realised success. And the day did come when he gave up smoking. Today even if he moves in the company of chain smokers, he is never tempted.

Never feel that you are a failure. Rather believe that you are on the way to success.

Where Are Their Mothers?

I read about a fashionable, rich young woman, who was taken around a poor locality of New York city. She was disgusted at the sight of the shabbily dressed, unkempt children on the streets.

"Look at these dreadful children!" she sneered. "Why can't someone wash and clean them up? Do they have no mothers?"

Her guide explained to her patiently, "Sure, they have mothers who love them – but they don't hate the dirt. You hate the dirt – but you don't love these children. Until the love for the children and hatred for their condition are found together in the same heart, the children will have to remain as they are!"

A Conqueror's Attitude

When William the Conqueror landed in Hastings and stepped on English soil, he stumbled and fell. This was regarded as an ill omen by his soldiers who let out a cry of dismay. But William was a man of tremendous optimism.

"What a wonderful thing has happened," he exclaimed. "I have already seized the land with both my hands." These words of the great conqueror were greeted with a loud cheer by his soldiers who now marched forward with redoubled enthusiasm.

William the Conqueror went on to make history.

Annie Besant Learns About the Law of *Karma*

When Dr. Annie Besant, the founder of the famous Theosophical Society of India, was a young woman, she worked on the editorial staff of a prestigious magazine called *The New Review*. She was an intellectual woman, given to mature reflection and logical thinking.

She gave birth to a baby, who fell seriously ill soon after birth. The baby was running high fever, and as the temperature rose, the infant developed convulsions. Annie Besant was distraught at the sight of her little child going through these violent fits. She could not bear to think of her innocent baby being put through such suffering.

"They say God is all Mercy and Love," she said to herself. "Is this the kind of mercy and love He shows my child? What has this tender, innocent babe done to deserve such suffering?"

She virtually gave up all faith and belief in God after this happened. She became an agnostic. She spoke to preachers and religious teachers. No one could answer her questions satisfactorily. "Where is God's love and compassion? Why is this child, who hasn't even hurt a fly, subject to such suffering?" They do not have an answer to such questions in Western philosophy, and Annie Besant got no answers.

One day, she came across a book by Mme. H. P. Blavatsky, entitled *Isis Unveiled*. The editor had sent it to her for the purpose of review. As Annie Besant began to read the book, a new understanding dawned on her, and she was deeply impressed by its contents. One of the chapters in the book was entitled, 'Karma and Reincarnation'. She read it again and again – and began to see life in a new perspective. She seemed to have found, at last, answers to the questions she had been asking. Here was the only satisfactory explanation for her innocent child's suffering: it was nothing but the result of the *karma* of the child's previous births!

Enlightenment came to her as in a flash of lightning. She understood that the present life was *not* the first life, the only life lived by her, or her child.

She had lived many, many, other lives before she had entered this body – likewise, her infant. It was due to the child's actions in those earlier births, that it was going through certain consequences in this birth. The infant had done something earlier, the effect of which, i.e., the fruit of which it was now faced with. The whole thing was crystal clear; the mystery was unravelled. She began to understand things, which were inexplicable earlier.

Because of this understanding, Annie Besant left her country, left behind her friends and family to come to India. She regarded India as the great land of the *rishis,* sages and saints who offered the most profound and satisfactory solution to life's problems. She came to live in Madras, and founded the famous Theosophical Society of India. There is a beautiful suburb of modern Chennai which is now named after her – Besant Nagar. India owes a deep debt of gratitude for all that Annie Besant has done, all the great services she rendered to this country. But she felt indebted to India for giving her a new insight into life and its meaning, through the doctrine of *karma* and reincarnation.

A Mirage

Napoleon's soldiers were marching across the African desert. They were famished by the heat, and overcome by thirst. As they trudged forward, someone from the fore ranks shouted, "Water! Here is water!"

Eagerly, the soldiers scanned the vast desert ahead. Far ahead of them, towards the horizon, they saw what appeared to be a lake. Its water shimmered and sparkled in the brilliant sunshine.

Mad with relief, the soldiers rushed forward in the direction of the 'water'. But as they raced towards it, it receded. To their utter dismay, that which seemed to be a lake of refreshing water was nothing but a mirage in the desert!

The illusory, passing, deceiving pleasures of this world too, are only a mirage – a vision of *maya*.

For the Love of My Brothers

Many of us have heard of Dr Albert Schweitzer – one of the greatest men of the twentieth century. He held three doctorates – a doctorate in Theology, a doctorate in Philosophy and a doctorate in Music. He worked as the Principal of a college, affiliated to the University of Strasbourg in Germany. He had written books, which had won for him international fame and critical acclaim. At the age of 32, he was struck by a sudden realisation: "All that I have done so far, I have done for myself," he thought. "What have I done for the love of God? What have I done in the service of suffering humanity?"

He began to look at the world from this new perspective, and soon enough he realised that in the "dark continent" of Africa, as it was called at that time, thousands of black people were suffering without medical aid. There were no doctors, who were ready to go out and serve them in the remote and inaccessible areas where they lived.

His mind was made up. This renowned and respected scholar gave up his job to become a medical student to acquire a fourth doctorate – this time, a doctorate in Medicine. Having become a full-fledged doctor, he went on to live in the backwoods of Africa, in Lamberene, to serve the poor black people there.

He was practically alone. He carried on his work – healing and helping the people. In his spare time, he set about building a hospital. He would go to the forest and fell down the trees, chop the wood and carry the timber to the site of the hospital on his shoulders. Toiling all by himself, log by log, he single-handedly endeavoured to raise the walls of the hospital building.

One day, struggling with a particularly heavy load, which he could not manage, he spotted a black man lounging nearby.

He requested the man, "Brother, can you give me a helping hand with this load?"

"Hey Mister," came the haughty reply, "don't you know I am educated?"

Dr Schweitzer smiled and said, "I am happy I am not educated!"

There was a great man who taught us how to serve with humility!

Many of Dr Schweitzer's friends felt that he was throwing away his talents and training, to no purpose. Some of them travelled to Africa to persuade him to come back to his native land. "Why should you work here among these black people?" they asked him. "What can a great and gifted man like you get out of all this hard labour?"

Schweitzer replied, "What does it matter where I live, provided I can do good work there? I appreciate your concern for me – but I have made up my mind to stay here and look after my African friends."

In fact, Dr Schweitzer remained in Africa, until he died in 1965, at the age of ninety. He worked until the end, serving the people who needed his help.

This is what true service is all about!

The Wheel of *Karma*

The *puranas* tell us a memorable tale of a king who wished to control his own destiny. He approached a saint and said to him, "O Holy One! You are a *trikaal gnani* – the past, the present and the future hold no secrets from you. I beg you to tell me what the future holds in store for me."

"Tell me, O King," said the saint, "what do you hope to gain from knowledge of your future?"

"If I know the worst that can happen to me, surely I can take steps to prevent the inevitable, the untoward incidents that may befall me," the King replied.

"If I tell you, King," the saint warned, "try as you might, you cannot prevent that which is to happen."

"I beg to differ," the King retorted. "If I know the worst, you and I together can work to prevent harm befalling me. Between us, we will surely find a way."

"So be it," said the saint. "I shall now begin to relate the events of your future. And with it, I offer you this challenge – you cannot prevent what is to happen, however hard you may try."

"Let me begin with this moment. Today is Thursday. Next Wednesday, someone will present you with a magnificent horse. I request you now, *not* to accept the horse for any reason. But I must also tell you, you will not be able to refuse it. You will accept it.

"The next day, you will ride the horse into the forest, reaching where the road runs in two directions. I warn you here and now, *do not* turn left; take the right turn. But I know that you will take the left turn and ride farther.

"Down the road, you will come across a beautiful woman, in deep distress and sorrow, who will implore you for help. I must urge you, O King, *not* to take pity on this woman, not even to cast a glance in her direction, and simply ride on. But I know for certain that you will not heed this warning. You will alight from the horse to offer help to the woman.

"Having offered to help the distressed woman, let me implore you not to go further. *Do not* allow her charms to ensnare you. However, I know that you will not be able to resist her beauty. You will take her with you and make her your queen.

"Soon thereafter, the queen will get you to perform a special *yagna*. O King, *by no means* must you consent to her wishes and undertake to perform the *yagna*. But alas, I know that you will go ahead and do exactly as she says.

"During the *yagna*, a young brahmin will appear before you and seek your permission to participate in the proceedings. Having ignored my warnings all along, King, pay heed to this one at least – *do not* grant permission to this young man to take part in the *yagna*.

"Alas, he will go ahead and participate in your *yagna*. In the course of the *yagna*, he will begin to mock at you and your queen. I warn you, O King, to guard your temper at that juncture, for your own good.

"I know for certain, that *you will fail* to control your anger, and in a fit of rage, you will kill the young brahmin. And the terrible sin of *brahmahathya* will alight on you! And your strong and handsome body will be covered with leprous sores! You will be liberated from this predicament when you hear the story of the *Mahabharata* with deep reverence and devotion.

"I have spoken," concluded the saint, "and I have warned you of the dangers. But you *cannot* escape your *Karma*."

The king grew thoughtful, and was determined to heed the saint's warnings at every juncture that was crucial. Forewarned is fore-armed, he thought to himself. With prior knowledge, he felt he would be able to alter events and circumstances.

Everything came to pass, just as the saint had predicted. Such was the power of his *prarabdha karma*, that at no point was the king able to act as per the saint's instructions. At each turn, he made the wrong decision. Events followed one another, until the prognosticated *yagna* came about, and the young brahmin provoked him beyond endurance. In a desperate, last ditch effort, the king tried to control his rage. But failing utterly he killed the young brahmin in a fit of rage, contracting the dreaded sin of *brahmahathya*.

The effect of *prarabdha karma* then, is inescapable, no matter how hard we try to evade its consequences. Only two choices are open to us – to accept whatever happens in a spirit of faith, and to bear it cheerfully; or to resist it, protest against our fate and spend our life in misery. We cannot change our *prarabdha karma* – but we can, in fact we must change our attitude to life.

Have We Forgotten Prayer?

There was a time when it was felt that only the illiterate, the uneducated women, dreamers, preachers and impractical people were interested in prayer. As for educated, intelligent people, people with 'rational' minds and advanced intellects, they certainly did not believe in prayer!

A few decades ago, a leading church magazine actually published the following obituary notice for prayer:

> Mrs. Prayer Meeting died recently at the First Neglected Church … For the past several years, Sister Prayer Meeting has been failing in health, gradually wasting away until rendered helpless by stiffness of knees, coldness of heart, inactivity, and weakness of purpose… The Post-mortem showed that a deficiency of spiritual food coupled with lack of faith, heartfelt religion and general support, were contributing causes. Only a few were present at her death, sobbing over memories of her past beauty and power.

The great statistician, Babson, once said: "The greatest undeveloped resource of the world is faith. And the greatest unused power is prayer."

True, prayer is a tremendous power – but, alas, it is an unused power.

I think of another great scientist, a Nobel Laureate, Dr. Alexis Carrel, who wrote a beautiful book called *The Human Destiny*. In it, Dr. Carrel says, "Prayer is the most powerful force that anyone can generate." The spiritual power of prayer, he tells us, is far greater than atomic energy. Dr. Carrel adds, "The world today, stands on the edge of destruction, because people have forgotten to pray."

Ticket to Heaven

Dharm Vir was a holy man who spent his life in devotion to the Lord and in the service of the poor. As he approached the end of his earthly days, he was blessed with a vision of the life hereafter – a vision of heaven and hell.

He saw the splendours of the heaven-world – the calm, the peace and tranquillity, and, above all, the great joy of dwelling at the Lotus feet of the Lord.

But he was shocked and pained at the vision of hell. He was deeply saddened by the plight of the lost souls, who were paying the price for their past sins.

"O Lord, save these poor souls," he prayed fervently. "If I have done any good *karma* in this life, may it all be used to rescue these souls in despair, and grant them the gift of the heaven-world."

Shortly afterwards, death came to the holy man. To his surprise, an angel had come to escort him to the heaven-world.

"But ... but ... I have given away the benefit of all my good *karma* to rescue those poor souls in distress! How can I then deserve the heaven-world?" he demanded of the angel.

"Oh pious one, the souls you have rescued from hell bless you for the grace you have bestowed on them," replied the angel. "Having attained heaven, they refuse to leave you behind! They pleaded with the Lord to have you among them."

Truly, compassion is the surest and safest way to heaven!

For the Love of God

There are a hundred and one ways of doing the same thing. Are you a professor teaching in a classroom? Are you a lawyer arguing a case in a court of law? Are you a doctor attending to patients? There are many ways of doing the same thing. Some are right, some are wrong. But only one is the best! And because you are doing everything for the love of God, because you are doing everything as an offering unto the Lord, you must do your work in the best way possible.

It was an Arabian poet who said: "Are you a mason building a house? Build it in the aspiration that some day perhaps the Beloved will come and dwell in your home. How much love would you not put into the building of such a house!

"Are you a weaver working at the loom, weaving a piece of cloth? Weave the cloth in the hope that the cloth will be worn by the Beloved. How much love would you not pour into your weaving!"

There was a painter who painted pictures of fascinating beauty. One day as he was painting, a friend happened to drop in. The artist was painting a beautiful portrait of Sri Krishna. The friend stood spellbound. The painting captivated his heart.

"Do you like the picture?" enquired the artist.

"Yes, I not only like but I admire the picture. You could not have painted such a beautiful face of the

Lord until you loved Him!" said the friend, with deep admiration.

"Love Him!" echoed the artist, "Of course I do. And the more I love Him, the better will I paint Him and the more fascinating will the picture become!"

It Was a Silent Prayer!

A father took his small son with him to run some errands. When it was time for lunch, they went to a local restaurant for a bite to eat. When their lunch was placed on the table, the father reminded the son, "We'll have a silent prayer."

The father finished praying first and waited for the little boy to complete his prayer. But the boy just sat there, his head bowed and his eyes closed. It was quite a while before he finally looked up.

"That was a long prayer," said the father. "What were you saying to God?"

"How do I know?" said the boy, in all innocence. "It was a silent prayer."

Turn to God

If you really want to succeed in life, you must contact the Source of success – God. God is the Source of success. So many people come and say to me: "We have done our best. But why have we failed? Why have we not succeeded in life?"

I narrate to them the story of a little boy who was walking on the road, with his father beside him. The son found a huge stone lying in the middle of the road, and he said to his father, "I want to remove this stone, lest some pedestrian should trip on it and get hurt."

"Go ahead son," said the father.

The little boy tried to lift up the stone. He struggled hard; he perspired; he put in his very best. But try as he might, he could not lift the stone. Dejected and frustrated, he said to his father, "I have put forth my best efforts, but I have failed."

"Where have you put forth your best efforts?" asked the father. "Here have I been standing by your side all the time. All that you needed to do was to turn to me and ask me to help you. And my strength would be your strength. In that added strength, you could have effortlessly lifted that stone."

Our Heavenly Father is always by our side. All we have to do is turn to Him for help and He will never fail us.

Doing Away with Ego

A young man was much given to pride and arrogance. He received a medal in the college, and it only added to his massive ego.

The man who bestowed the medal on him used extravagant language to praise him and his accomplishments.

The young man's head and heart were swollen with pride.

That night, when he went home, he repeated the words of praise he received, to his mother. Having delivered a glowing tribute to himself, he asked her, "How many great men are there in the world today, anyhow?"

The mother, a wise old woman, looked at him with pity and said, "One less than you think!"

Truly, our ego can blind us to the truth about ourselves.

A proud lawyer told a farmer, "I never bow my head before anyone – neither God nor man!"

The wise farmer replied, "Can you see that field of grain? Only the heads of grain that are empty, stand upright. The well-filled ones bow low!"

A proud lady arrived late at a concert and found that she could be seated only in one of the back rows, for the hall was full.

Angry and insulted, she said to the organisers, "You obviously do not know how to seat your guests properly!"

"Not at all, madam," said one of them, "those who matter don't mind where they sit. Those who mind, do not really matter!"

Dissociate yourself from the ego. Until you have liberated yourself from this false identification, you will continue to be in bondage.

The Value of *Satsang*

An ancient legend tells us a memorable story about the power of *satsang*. Once, Rishi Narada approached Lord Vishnu and requested him humbly: "My Lord! Do tell me about the value and influence of *satsang*. I am eager to know what it can do for the seeker."

Lord Vishnu smiled at Narada. He said, "I am so busy now, I do not have the time to talk to you about it. But I would like to help you. Please go to the giant *banyan* tree in the forest located at the foot of the Meru Hills. There you will find a squirrel. He will enlighten you about *satsang*."

Rishi Narada was puzzled. A squirrel – to enlighten him on *satsang!* But the Lord's word was absolute, and Narada did as he was told. He found the tree in question, and a lively squirrel jumped down before him.

With all respect, Narada said to him, "I pray you, dear squirrel, enlighten me on the value and influence of *satsang*."

The squirrel looked at Narada with its beady, bright eyes for what seemed to be a long drawn out minute. Narada looked into its eyes and held his gaze. At the end of the minute the squirrel curled up, lifeless. It was dead!

Taken aback, Narada found his way back to *Vaikunth*, where he narrated the moving incident to the Lord. "I hope I have not been instrumental in the death of the poor creature," he lamented. "And, dear Lord, my question is still unanswered. Wilt Thou enlighten me?"

"I'm afraid that's not possible Narada," replied the Lord. "Go back to the same tree. You will find a monkey, who will give you the knowledge you seek."

Faithfully, Narada did as he was told. Indeed, he found the monkey swinging from one branch to another. When he saw Narada, the monkey jumped down with a thud.

"I pray you, O monkey, to enlighten me on the value of *satsang*," Narada said to the monkey respectfully.

The monkey drew close and looked deep into Narada's eyes. In a minute, he dropped dead at the rishi's feet.

This time, Narada was nonplussed. In utter shock, he rushed to Lord Vishnu and said: "Lord, I do not know what is wrong. The monkey you mentioned has also dropped dead before my eyes. What am I doing to these poor creatures? Who will now enlighten me on *satsang?*"

"Well, Narada," said Lord Vishnu. "Tomorrow a prince will be born in the royal family of the kingdom in which the forest is located. Go and bless the new born child, and he will enlighten you on the matter you seek."

"But … my Lord … " stammered Narada. "When I consider the fate of the squirrel … and the monkey… how can I dare to approach this innocent, newborn baby?"

"Do you or don't you need enlightenment on *satsang?*" asked the Lord with a smile. "Go to the child. Your quest will be fulfilled."

It was with a trembling heart that Narada entered the royal palace the next morning. The King and

Queen were deeply honoured to see him. They welcomed him with all ceremony that was due to a *maharishi*. They entreated him to bless their newborn son – the heir to the throne.

Rishi Narada was taken to the room where the baby prince lay asleep in the cradle. His heart beat fast as he laid his hand on the brow of the child to bless him.

No sooner had he touched the child, than the baby opened its eyes and looked deep into the eyes of the Rishi.

"O Prince," said Rishi Narada, a cold sweat breaking out over his forehead. "Lord Vishnu bade me come to you to ask you about the value of *satsang*."

To the rishi's utter amazement, the baby began to speak. "Rishi Narada, you see me here – the manifest proof of the value of *satsang*. In my previous births, I was a squirrel, and then a monkey. As a squirrel, I was only motivated by appetite. I did nothing but gather and hoard. When I met you and looked into your eyes, I was released from that birth. My *karma* caused me to take birth as a monkey. Then again, I had the good fortune to encounter you at close quarters. Released from that incarnation, I have risen in the scale of evolution to take birth as a Prince in the pious family of the King of this country. If one minute in the company of a holy one like you could help me this far, I leave you to judge what the value and influence of sustained *satsang* can be!"

Rishi Narada was overjoyed. The Lord had indeed performed a *leela* to teach his humble devotee the value of *satsang*.

Walking 'The Little Way'

My beloved master, Sadhu Vaswani, urged all of us to walk 'the little way'. To illustrate what he meant by 'the little way', he narrated the following story to us.

A man had a dream in which he dreamt that he stood at the gates of Paradise. He saw various blessed souls in his dream, approaching the golden gates and demanding admittance to the heaven world.

The first to knock on the golden gates was a learned *pundit*. "Let me enter," he said to the Angel guarding the portals of paradise. "I have studied the holy scriptures day and night, and I have earned the right to enter heaven."

"Wait!" said the Angel. "We shall look at our earthly records to see if you studied the scriptures in reverence for the Lord, or for the sake of social applause and admiration."

The next to appear at the gate was a holy man. "Allow me to enter," he said to the Angel. "I have fasted much."

"Wait," said the Angel. "We shall first enquire if your motives were pure."

Then came a man, simple as simple can be. He asked in humility, "May I be allowed to enter within?"

"Tell me what you have done with your life," the Angel demanded of him.

The man said hesitantly, "A few fragments of my bread I shared each day with a brother who limped, and could not earn his daily food. I swept his floor and filled his water jug every day. And I prayed to the Lord, 'Dear God, make me a servant of those who suffer, and are in pain!'"

To him the Angel said, "Blessed among mortals art thou! Walking the little way, thou hast attained the Abode of the Immortals! The gates of Heaven are open unto thee!"

Avali's Wrath

Countless are the legends that have grown around Sant Tukaram, the simple-minded, pure-hearted, great-souled, poet-saint of Maharashtra.

Rukmani, the consort of Lord Vithal wished to see for herself Tuka's kindness to the humble and lowly. Assuming the form of a poor woman, she came to Tuka's door and begged for a *sari*, for she had only rags to wear. His heart melting at the tears of the poor woman, Tuka promptly gave her a *sari* belonging to his wife, Avali.

Avali, who was returning home from the river, saw the stranger walking away with her *sari*. Reaching home she demanded suspiciously of her husband, "Who was that woman at our door?"

"My dear Avali," began Tuka. "You should have seen the condition of that poor sister! She had no decent clothes to wear! My heart was touched – so would yours, Avali, had you been here at the time!"

"Never mind that!" said Avali sharply. "Just tell me, did you or did you not give her my green *sari?*"

"As a matter of fact I did," agreed Tuka. "It was for the love of Vithal, He who regards the poor as His own..."

"You and your Vithal!" said Avali with gritted teeth. "I've had enough of Him! And I intend to let Him know what I think of Him, too!"

In her wrath and frustration, she picked up a heavy stone pestle – a grinding stone – from her kitchen and made her way to the temple at Pandarpur. Her intention was to break the image of Lord Vithobha, whom she blamed for reducing her husband to folly and indigence.

Lo and behold! When she reached the temple she was stunned to see Goddess Rukmani clad in her favourite green *sari!* The pestle fell from her hands and she bowed down with tear-filled eyes at the feet of the Divine Couple who had made her play a part in their *leela!* She shed tears of bitter repentance, begging the Lord's forgiveness – and when she raised her eyes, she found herself sparkling with gold and silver, clad in a silk *sari!*

The Lord gives, gives and ever gives – though we are apt to imagine that He takes away from us!

Ty Cobb's Batting Average

A broken, tired, defeated man went to see his Rabbi, seeking comfort and guidance in his deep despair.

"Help me, Rabbi!" he cried. "I'm so tired of failing. Nothing I try ever seems to work, what should I do?"

"I'll tell you what to do," said the Rabbi. "Go and look up page seven hundred and twenty of the World Almanac."

The man went to the library, located the book and turned to page seven hundred and twenty. He found a list of the batting averages of the great baseball players of the world. At the top of page was the name of Ty Cobb, the greatest slugger of all time. His average was three hundred and sixty seven.

Puzzled, the man went back to the Rabbi. "I don't understand," he said. "What am I supposed to learn from Ty Cobb's batting average?"

"He was the greatest of them all," said the Rabbi. "His average was three hundred and sixty seven which means – one out of every three times he stood at the plate, he got a hit. But two out of every three times, he *did not* get a hit. And he was the greatest."

Life is not simply a matter of victory. We fail, we fail and we fail, until finally, we succeed. There are always going to be discouraging times when we will want to give up, and walk away from it all. But perseverance is that voice inside you, which says, "Never, never, never give up!"

Listen to this voice, if you wish to succeed!

The Best Kind of Prayer

A poor farmer, returning home from the market after a long tiring day, found that the wheel of his cart was about to come loose. He was in the middle of the woods, and his cart was loaded with produce.

Anxiously, he searched his pockets for the little prayer book, which he always carried with him. To his dismay he found that he had forgotten to bring it with him.

He closed his eyes and began to pray thus: "Dear God, I have done something very foolish. I have left my prayer book at home, and my memory is not what it used to be. I don't seem to remember a single prayer. So this is what I am going to do. I shall recite the alphabet – very, very slowly – several times. Since you know all the prayers, please put the letters together and form the right prayer for me!"

The Lord said: "This prayer is the best I have heard today – for it came from a heart that is simple, pure and sincere!"

Doing Our Best

In a certain cotton factory, a notice was put up on the walls of the workroom. It read as follows: *If your threads get tangled, send for the foreman.*

One day a new worker got her threads tangled. She tried to disentangle them, but only made them worse. Then she sent for the foreman.

He arrived quietly and looked at her threads. "You have been trying to do this yourself?" he asked her.

"Yes," she replied.

"But why did you not send for me? Those were the instructions."

"I was doing my best," she said.

"No, you were not," the foreman said. "Remember that doing your best is sending for me!"

How often do we act like this worker! When we are in trouble, we often make things worse for ourselves. We run from pillar to post, appealing for help. We turn to our relatives; we entreat our friends for their support; we knock at the doors of our bank manager; we appeal to our business associates. We are only making things worse. We should call upon God for help, for that is the best thing we can do!

Just a Minute!

There is a story of a man who prayed to God, "God, please grant me a million dollars instantly. What is a million to You? In the infinity of Your abundance, a million dollars is no more than a cent. So send me a million dollars at once, please!"

The story goes that this man hears a voice. It is the Voice of God, which tells him, "My child, I am ready to give you one million dollars. It shall be given to you in one minute. You will have to wait one minute. And, in the vastness of my eternity, one minute is just a million years. So just wait for a million years, and you will get your million dollars!"

The Happy Peasant

A king set out in disguise to discover for himself, the happiest man in his kingdom.

Having met hundreds of people, at long last he came across a poor peasant, singing happily as he

tilled the soil. There was such a radiant joy on his face that the king was drawn irresistibly towards him.

"Dear friend," he said to the peasant. "Tell me the secret of your joy."

"It's very simple, really," said the peasant. "One-fourth of what I earn, I repay as the debt I owe; one-fourth, I invest in the future; one-fourth, I give away in charity and one-fourth, I spend on my duty."

The king was thoroughly bewildered. He begged the peasant to explain further.

"My parents gave me the great gift of life, and I owe them a deep debt of gratitude. I now cherish them and look after them in their old age. One-fourth of my income is thus spent in repaying my debt.

"My children represent the future. I spend one-fourth of my income on feeding, clothing and educating them. This is my investment in the future.

"Poor though I am, there are people worse off than me. I help them as much as I can, and one-fourth of my income is spent on charity.

"My wife has placed her trust in me. It is my duty to love and protect her till the end of my life. One-fourth of my income is spent on giving her a good home.

"This is the secret of my happiness!"

The king was beginning to do his own mental arithmetic. He began to make plans for the division of his own vast wealth. To start with, he rewarded the peasant richly, indeed!

Compassion First

Swami Vivekananda put forward the highest concept of service when he coined the term *Daridranarayana* – the Lord in the form of the poor – and asked people to serve Him. "Where would you go to seek God?" he asked. "Are not all the poor, the miserable, the weak, Gods? Why not worship them first?"

Swamiji had the compassionate heart of a mother. When a famine was raging in Bengal and his followers could not get money to carry out relief work, he seriously thought of selling the Belur Math property, which he had just purchased to set up the spiritual centre of the Ramakrishna Mission.

So intense was his compassion, and spirit of service that he once said to a friend, "The thought comes to me that even if I have to undergo a thousand births to relieve the misery of the world, aye, even to remove the least pain from anyone, I shall cheerfully do it. Of what use is my personal *mukti* alone? I shall take everyone along that path with myself!"

Money Can't Buy Happiness

Everyone wants to be successful in life. But there are few who know the elements of success, the factors that go to build up success. Today, success is being confounded with making money, with amassing millions and billions. John D. Rockefeller was such a multimillionaire, to whom success did not bring happiness. His biographer tells us that by the time Rockefeller was 53, his life was a wreck. He was the richest man in the world and yet he was miserable! He was sick – physically, mentally and emotionally. All his millions could not make him happy.

Rockefeller turned a new leaf. He stopped accumulating wealth, and began to give away his wealth. Thus was born the Rockefeller Foundation, which sponsors and supports education and medical care throughout the world. John Rockefeller rewrote and redefined the meaning of success for himself.

Let the Mind Be Pure!

An anxious disciple went to a spiritual master and said, "A deep desire has arisen within me for God-realisation. Pray, show me the way to *mukti* – liberation. Grant me the gift of emancipation."

The guru quietly replied, "In order to fulfil your wish, you will have to come and stay for a period of time with me, follow my instructions and surely you will attain enlightenment."

"This is the jet age," the disciple interrupted, "The computer age. Why can't you give me enlightenment right now?"

The guru thought for a moment and said to him, "I am glad you are eager to receive enlightenment. Let us first try to get a little familiar with each other. If you will permit me, tonight I will come and have dinner with you."

The aspirant jumped at the idea. At night the guru arrived at the residence of the aspirant.

Immediately he said to the aspirant, "I am eager to eat. Kindly put all the dishes you have cooked into my begging bowl."

The aspirant looked into the begging bowl and saw that it already had some stale, leftover articles of food.

"Let me wash the bowl first," he said.

"I am too hungry. I cannot wait. Forget about washing the bowl, be quick and serve me with the food," the guru insisted.

"But I have made everything with so much effort. Great care has been taken to cook a delicious meal for you. The good food will get polluted if it is put in this filthy, unwashed bowl!"

Quietly answered the guru: "If this food can't be served until the vessel is clean, how can I put enlightenment – the food of knowledge – into your mind which is not pure? First purify the mind through the practice of silence!"

The Prayer of Denial

There was a notorious thief and murderer. He would set out every night, stop innocent travellers, murder them and loot their possessions. He was utterly ruthless, utterly pitiless.

One night, he caught hold of a *rishi*, and was about to kill him. The *rishi* looked at him with compassion and asked him, "Dear brother, are you aware that your day of reckoning is drawing near?"

"What day of reckoning?" growled the dacoit.

"A day of reckoning comes in the life of every one of us," explained the *rishi*. "You will have to face the Lord. You must account for all your actions. You must justify every act, every deed you have done in your life. How will you account for the countless thefts and murders you have committed? What will be your answer to the Lord?"

The thief laughed out aloud. "I am not alone! I am not answerable on my own account. I have done all this only for the sake of my old parents, my wife and children. They will answer for me. They will account for my actions."

The *rishi* said to him, "Go to your wife now. Ask her whether she will be answerable for your actions. Ask your old parents and your children whether they will stand by you on your day of reckoning."

Instantly, the thief rushed to his house and roused his wife and children from their slumber. He told them of the conversation he had had with the *rishi*. "I have become a thief and murderer for your sake," he declared passionately. "I have done all that I have done only to protect you, feed you and clothe you. Will you or will you not answer for me on my day of reckoning?"

His wife looked him in the eye and replied, "What have we got to do with your misdeeds? You say you did it all to protect us. But we never asked you to kill and loot! We never asked you to plunder and murder! So why should we answer for you on your day of reckoning? All that you have done is your own responsibility – we shall not share in your sins and misdeeds. They will come down on your head – yours alone!" Similar was the reaction of his parents and children.

Disillusioned, the thief returned to the *rishi* and fell at his feet. "Save me, O man of God," he begged. "I am answerable for my own actions. Tell me how I must face God; tell me how I can plead for His Mercy."

Then it was that the *rishi* taught him the power of the prayer of denial. This is the prayer by which we deny the thoughts and feelings that cause us incalculable harm. This prayer helps us to deny the experiences that dwarf and degrade our life. "From now on, my brother," he explained, "you must learn to say no to every temptation, every evil impulse that crosses your mind. You must practise the prayer of denial to put an end to all your evil deeds."

So saying, the *rishi* blessed him and told him to utter a *mantra* which he gave him. "Keep on repeating this *mantra*," he said. "It will cleanse your soiled heart and wash it whiter than snow."

Transformed and chastened, the dacoit went into a trance, and began to utter the name that was given to him. He was lost to all thoughts of the world. He grew indifferent to hunger, thirst and bodily demands. He gave himself up to the Name Divine ...

Through the power of the prayer of denial, the criminal was transformed and became a divine seer and sage.

Be Like the Tiger, Not the Fox!

A man was walking through a forest, and came across a fox which had lost its legs. He wondered how the animal could survive in such a state.

Soon thereafter, he saw a tiger coming to the same place with game in its mouth. The tiger ate its fill, leaving the rest for the fox.

The man observed the fox for a few days. Every day he saw that God sent the tiger to feed the fox. The man was struck with the wonder that was God's providence. He decided, "I too shall be like the fox. I shall lie in a corner, trusting the Lord to give me all I need!"

He did this for a month. And sure enough, he was close to death when a voice whispered in his ear: "You are on the path of error! Open your eyes to the truth! Be like the tiger, not the fox!"

Let us do our duty. God will do His! When Jesus urged his disciples to be like the lilies of the field, he did not mean that they should give up on their duty. He only urged them not to give in to constant worry and care.

We all know the wonderful proverb, "God helps those who help themselves". Let us therefore continue to do our duty; God will take care of the rest.

A pious man saw a naked child on a street, hungry and shivering in the cold. He became angry and said to God, "How can You allow such a thing to happen? Why can't You do something about this?"

God's answer came to him, loud and clear: "I certainly did something. I made you!"

The Suitor of Wales

There is an amusing story told to us, of a man who is known as the Suitor of Wales. This man lived in Wales, and when he was very young, he fell in love with a young woman of his acquaintance. He could not pick up the guts to go and propose to her. He was too timid, too shy. So he decided to write a letter to her.

The letter was written and delivered. But he did not get an answer. So he wrote her a second letter. That too, elicited no reply from his beloved. He kept writing to her, again and again. How many letters do you think he wrote in all? You will be surprised, he wrote in all 2,148 letters! By then, he was seventy years old, and so was she! Strangely enough, both were still unmarried. So finally, he summoned enough courage to go and propose to her. And the woman finally accepted, and they were both married at the grand old age of seventy-three! He never, never, never gave up!

Are We Really Free?

Sri Ramakrishna Paramahansa was brilliant at illustrating the most profound and complex truths of life by means of beautiful and simple parables. One day he said to his disciples: "Every day, fishermen cast their wide nets into the sea. A few fish are caught in the net. Many escape. Those that have escaped the net, swim about freely in the ocean; indeed, some fish are never ever caught. But those that are caught in the net, struggle to escape; and some of them actually succeed. They leap so valiantly, that they free themselves from the net, and get back into the vast and deep waters of the sea, where lies their true home. There are other fish caught in the net who also struggle to be free – but in vain. In vain they seek a way out, for someone to free them from the death-trap that ensnares them. They struggle persistently.

"But there are a few fish who are blissfully ignorant, happily unaware of their condition. They are content to rest passively in the net that ensnares them, unaware of the terrible and painful fate that awaits them."

In this significant parable, Sri Ramakrishna refers to the human condition; especially to the four kinds of people – the *nityamukta*, those who are not touched by the bonds of *karma;* the *mukta*, those who, through their own efforts and the grace of God, liberate themselves from the bonds of *karma;* third, those who seek liberation and are struggling for it constantly; fourth, those who are so entrapped in their worldly life that they are unaware of their own bondage and seek nothing!

Only a Woodcutter

There was a man who met me. He said to me, "I do not believe in God. I do not believe in prayers. I have never ever prayed to God even once in all my life."

I asked him, "Are you sure you have never prayed to God even once in all your life?"

He thought for a few moments and said, "Yes, I remember I offered a prayer once."

He paused to reflect a while.

"When I was a little boy," he said, "I had lost my way in a forest. I ran here and there, I shouted for help. I was terrified! Scared and shivering, in that desperate mood, I cried out, 'Oh God, if You really exist, show me the way out of this place. Let me reach home safely'."

"What happened then?" I urged him.

"Nothing," he said.

"That's not possible," I said gently. "How could nothing have happened? Surely something must have happened, or you wouldn't be here before me. You must have found your way back to your house on that fateful day. God must have heard your prayer, surely."

"No," denied the man vehemently. "He did not come to my help. I was so scared I sat down under a tree and just cried. God did not hear me, I tell you! But a woodcutter came along. He happened to be

passing by, and he told me he felt an urge to walk through that part of the forest. So there he was. He took my hand and led me out of the forest. It was only a woodcutter who saved me. Not God!"

"Only a woodcutter!" I exclaimed. "What do you expect God to look like? Did you expect a man in white flowing garments with a long beard? Did you not realise that He heard your prayer and came to your rescue in the form of a woodcutter?"

A Friend Indeed!

A holy man of God was being shown around a new and impressive hospital complex, which had just been completed. It was fitted with the latest and most sophisticated equipments. No efforts had been spared to offer patients the best care possible.

The holy man was shown a button placed by the bedside of each patient. "This is indeed special," the Director of the hospital explained. "In most hospitals, the patient presses a button, which rings a bell, to call an attendant or a nurse. Often, the bell was not heard. Or, if it was, sometimes the staff were confused by various bells, and some patients were not attended to. But now, at the touch of even the weakest patient, this button makes four lights flash – one at the nursing station, one above his bed, one in the corridor and one in the ward sister's room. The lights can be turned off only when the call has been answered, and the patient has been visited!"

The holy man smiled. "Human ingenuity has indeed devised a wonderful scheme to help those in need," he remarked. "How much more wonderful must God's scheme be! Surely He hears the cries of His weakest children! When the weakest hand touches the button of prayer, there is no power on earth which can hinder the signal, or bar the answer!"

The Smell of Money

Lala Ramchand's sweet shop occupied pride of place in the High Street of Rampur town. The enticing display of sweetmeats and other delectable eats drew crowds of buyers to Lala's shop. And a delicious flavour of *ghee*, sugar, *keshar* and *elaichi* wafted out from the kitchen at the back, where culinary experts toiled over the hot fire to produce the sweets that Lala Ramchand's shop was renowned for.

Ranga was a poor labourer who lived in Rampur. He worked as a coolie for daily wages in the wholesale vegetable market adjacent to the High Street. Everyday he would pass by Lala's shop, and cast a longing glance at the mounds of sweets and the people who were eagerly dipping into freshly bought packets of sweets and savouries. Poor Ranga! He would swallow hard, even as he salivated at the sight of those sweets! But none knew better than he that such delicacies were not for the likes of him. The few coins he earned were barely enough to provide one meal for him and his old parents. As for Lala's sweets – they would remain a pipe-dream for ever!

Every day Ranga's mother packed two dry *rotis*, along with a green chilly, an onion and a piece of lime. This was his midday meal. He and his fellow coolies would snatch a few minutes of rest from their hard labour as they ate their lunch.

One afternoon, as Ranga looked for a shady place to sit, he caught sight of a stone bench under a tree just outside Lala's shop. Usually the bench was always occupied by shopkeepers or passers-by; but now it was nearly 3 o'clock in the afternoon – the siesta hour – and the High Street wore a deserted look. Ranga sat on the bench, resting his weary limbs at long last, and opened his lunch packet.

Suddenly, the most delicious smell of spices, flour, potatoes and hot oil wafted in his direction. Of course, it was from Lala Ramchand's kitchen, where preparations were on to stock up on savouries like *samosas* and *kachoris* for the evening rush that would soon follow. As Ranga breathed deep, his eyes closed in ecstasy, for he could imagine how delicious those eats would be! Enjoying the mere smell as if he were actually tasting those savouries which he could never afford, Ranga began to eat his simple lunch. How delicious the dry *rotis* tasted that day! And when the humble repast was over, there was the heavenly smell of *burfi* and *halwa* in the air. Ranga felt as if he had a square meal, finishing off with a sweet for dessert.

From then on Ranga decided that he would repair to the stone bench every day to eat his lunch. It had to be a late lunch – but that was OK – because by then, the bench would be vacant, and the delectable smell from Lala Ramchand's kitchen would accompany his workaday meal, affording him a pleasure and thrill which did not cost any money!

And so Ranga continued with his practice of eating a late lunch outside Lala's shop, savouring the smell of the delicacies that wafted from the kitchen. The Lala noticed him on three separate occasions – breathing in those delicious vapours, his eyes closed, with a gratified look on his face, as if he had actually eaten a favourite dish. The Lala's eyes narrowed in anger. How dare this poor coolie take the smell from his famed kitchen for free?

The next day, as Ranga left the stone bench after his meal, the Lala beckoned to him. Ranga was astonished. He looked round to see if it was someone else the Lala was calling.

"You! It's you I want," said Lala imperiously.

Ranga's eyes widened. His heart raced. May be the Lala would give him a few leftovers or broken fragments of the sweets and snacks! Many rich shopkeepers did it, he knew. If that was so, Ranga decided, he would share the bounty with his fellow labourers, and take some home for his old parents. For never in their lifetime, could they ever afford to *buy* anything from Lala's sweetshop.

He approached Lala who was seated on a comfortable *divan* just inside the shop. He could barely take his eyes off the sweets which he was seeing at such close quarters for the very first time!

"So..." drawled Lala, "you are in the habit of sitting outside my shop and enjoying the smell from my kitchen?"

"I... yes, your honour!" Ranga stammered.

"*Nikalo paisa*," (Take out the money) demanded Lala in a menacing voice.

"Take out money?" said Ranga, flabbergasted. "But why? I haven't taken anything!"

"Oh yes you have," said Lala sternly. "You poor rogue, even the *smell* from my shop isn't for free! You have been sitting there day after day taking in that delicious smell? *Nikalo paisa* – I've seen you enjoying the smell. So pay up now!"

"Is there no justice?" wailed Ranga. "How should someone be expected to pay for *smelling* food?"

A small crowd gathered round the shop as one of Lala's burly servants caught hold of Ranga. "Pay up," he demanded menacingly.

"What has the fellow done, Lala?" someone wanted to know. "Has he stolen something from your shop?"

"No, but he has been smelling the vapours that float from my kitchen, and I insist on payment," replied Lala Ramchand.

A holy man who was passing by, heard Lala's reply and stepped forward.

"Here is the money," he said to Lala, holding out a hundred rupee note. "I shall pay for this poor man."

Lala's greedy hand stretched out eagerly to snatch the money. But the holy man tantalisingly drew back. As Lala stared, he brought his hand forward, holding the currency note close to Lala's face, waving it right and left.

Lala tried to snatch, but failed. "Give me the money," he demanded hoarsely.

"Give you the money? Oh no!" said the holy man. "This poor man has been *smelling* your food. You, in turn, can *smell* the money as due payment. That is all he owes you!"

The onlookers clapped and cheered, as the logic of the holy man's answer appealed to them greatly. "Yes, yes," they said in chorus. "He only *smelt* your food – so you can *smell* his money!"

Lala Ramchand was nonplussed. Ranga fell at the holy man's feet with tear-filled eyes.

I Offer Myself !

The story is about a missionary meeting held in Scotland where offerings were being collected from people for various service programmes that were being conducted all over the world. People gave generously – for their compassion had been stirred by the plight of the people who so desperately needed their help.

Alexander Duff, a little boy of ten, was present at the gathering. His heart had been touched too – but he had nothing to offer, not even the smallest coin. When the basket of offerings had been passed round, the volunteers were about to take it away, when little Alexander stopped them. "Please sir, lower the basket a little!" he pleaded.

The volunteers thought that the little boy had a whim, and obligingly put the basket on the floor. Imagine their surprise, when he stepped into the basket with folded hands, saying, "I have no money to give, but I would like to offer myself to the service of my brothers and sisters!"

Obeying Instructions

There was a servant whose master asked him to bring a few biscuits. The servant knew very little about etiquette. He brought the biscuits in his hand and gave them to his master.

The master was annoyed. "You stupid fellow," he exclaimed. "You must bring everything to me on a plate or a dish!"

The servant said meekly, "Yes master, I will do that. It's a very simple thing after all."

Some time later the master ordered the servant to bring his shoes. The servant promptly brought them on a plate. Enraged, the master shouted, "You stupid fellow, what are you doing?" The bewildered servant replied, "But sir, those were your instructions! I am only obeying your orders."

Our subconscious is like the servant. It cannot think for itself. It cannot decide what is right and what is wrong. It can only obey. It is up to us to give it the right direction!

The Spirit of Acceptance

There is a beautiful story told us in the *Mahabharata*. It is said that the God of the Ocean once said to River Ganga, "O Ganga! You bring with yourself huge banyan and oak trees as you flow into me. Why is it that you don't bring me some of those tender, delicate herbs that grow on your banks?"

The Ganga replied, "Those tender herbs you speak of may appear frail and weak, but, even though my water sweeps over them with force, they only bow down low before me, allowing me to flow past. Oaks and banyans, on the other hand, stand up against my flood, and I break them by their roots."

Egoistic defiance will only break you. On the other hand, humility and acceptance will give you the strength to resist adversity. If you bend, you cannot be broken!

O Ye of Little Faith!

There is an amusing story about a group of men, who came to a saint of God. "O holy man, help us!" they pleaded. "Our village has been struck by a severe drought. We beg you to pray with us, so that God may send the rain down at once. We are sure it will pour if you joined our prayers."

"When do you want to pray?" enquired the holy man.

"Right now," they answered. "Let us pray here and now. Let the Lord send down the rain forthwith."

The holy man said to them, "Where is your faith? You said you were sure that the Lord will answer our prayer; but where is the mark of that faith? Not one of you has brought an umbrella with you; not one of you has a raincoat. And yet you believe the rain will come down?"

It was Swami Vivekananda who said, "With His grace, we can cross the seven seas. But without His grace, we cannot even cross the threshold."

This is the kind of faith we need to sustain us through life.

The 'Man Eater'

A holy man who had conquered worldly desires was passing through a dark and thick jungle, when he saw a heap of looted treasure – silver, gold and precious jewels – that had been abandoned there, possibly by dacoits fleeing for their lives.

Aware of the lure of wealth for unscrupulous people, the holy man decided that his duty would be to find the right person who would use the ill-gotten loot in the service of the poor and the lowly. He prayed to God to send before him such a man, who would act as an instrument of benevolence and selfless service.

As he walked on in search of such a man, he met two merchants who were crossing the jungle along with their servant.

"You seem to be in such a hurry," one of them remarked, "What is it that you are running away from?"

The sage replied, "Deep inside this jungle is a strange beast. If it is not handled with care, it can turn out to be a man-eater! But, in the hands of a right person, it can also turn out to be a life-saver. I go in search of the right man."

Unable to understand the significance of the holy man's words, the merchants laughed scornfully at him, "Man-eater? We know how to handle a man-eater, for we are used to crossing the jungle! We are the right men to handle the man-eater. So you can be off on your way!" they said to him.

The holy man looked at them with pity and walked on. Some time later, he reached a clearing in the woods, where he found a man resting under the shade of a tree. At the sight of the sage, the man arose and bowed in reverence. He offered the sage water to drink and some fruits to eat.

The holy man blessed him and asked him, "Who are you, brother? And what brings you into this deep jungle?"

The man replied that his name was Karunakar, and that he had devoted his life to serving and helping the poor tribals who lived on the fringes of the jungle.

Their lot was indeed to be pitied – for no one cared for them and their welfare. It was his aspiration to build a school for their children, and, if possible, set up a *chikitshala* or hospital that would offer them medical care. So he had set out to visit the neighbouring cities and towns, to place his need before philanthropists and businessmen, who, he hoped, would offer him assistance to execute the project. But, alas, his efforts were in vain.

"A hospital and school for the tribals?" the wealthy men had sneered. "For centuries they have managed to live and die in their ignorance and hunger. Why are you trying to give them what they don't know and don't need? We have better things to do with our money than pour it down the drain on projects like these!"

Karunakar sighed as he said to the holy man, "And so, *swamiji*, I am returning empty-handed to my people. I cannot offer them anything but my own love and effort, and that I will continue to do, as long as I live."

The holy man smiled and said to him, "Deep inside the jungle is a strange beast. Depending on how you handle it, it can be a man-eater or a life-saver." He looked deeply into the eyes of Karunakar and added, "Perhaps you are the right man to handle it."

"If that is God's will, so be it," said Karunakar. He touched the holy man's feet and took his leave to resume his journey.

In the meanwhile the two merchants and their servant reached the spot where the looted treasure lay. Their eyes widened with greed at the sight of all the wealth. Prompted by avarice, each of them secretly plotted to do away with the other two, so that he and he alone, could possess all the wealth.

The two merchants bade their servant to cook some food while they went to bathe in the stream nearby. While they were taking their bath, one merchant pushed the other into the swirling waters and held him there, causing him to drown. The murderous merchant then crouched slowly up to the spot where the servant was cooking their meal. He stabbed the servant from behind, killing him instantly. Delighted with his own exploits, he sat down to eat the food. "All this wealth is now mine, and mine alone!" he said to himself, mightily pleased.

Unbeknown to him, the wily servant had poisoned the food he was cooking. He too, had wanted to keep the treasure for himself, and had planned to poison the merchants. As the murderer ate the poisoned food, he dropped dead.

When Karunakar arrived, he was appalled by the dreadful sight that met his eyes. The drowned merchant's lifeless body lay on the banks of the stream; the servant who had been stabbed to death was sprawled under a tree; their murderer lay dead, over the poisoned food he had consumed. The gleaming treasure was still there untouched.

"Ah!" sighed Karunakar. "So this was the beast that turned into a man-eater! I shall abide by the holy man's counsel, and turn it into a life-saver!"

Very soon thereafter, a school and a hospital were raised to serve the poor tribals who lived on the outskirts of the jungle. Other amenities were provided for them by their kind benefactor, Karunakar, who saw to it that every *paisa* of the treasure was spent in the benefit of his needy brothers and sisters.

Truly, in Karunakar's hands, the treasure proved to be a life-saver!

Let Nothing Block Your Horizon!

Robert Louis Stevenson, the famous writer, was a victim to chronic TB, suffering from the disease which wasted much of his life. But he would not allow the disease to get his spirits down. He would greet his wife every morning with the cheerful words, "Isn't it a wonderful day!"

One day, he was caught in a terrible bout of coughing. His wife said to him, "Do you still believe that it is a wonderful day?"

"Of course it is a wonderful day," Stevenson replied, turning to a window ablaze with sunlight. "I will never let a row of medicine bottles block my horizon."

Surely, we can all choose our attitude!

Do You Like What You Are Doing?

A General was visiting a platoon of paratroopers. Chatting with them after the formal inspection, he asked a few of them, "Do you like jumping out of planes?"

"I love it, sir!" replied the first paratrooper.

"How do you like jumping?" he asked the second one. "It's a fantastic experience sir!" exclaimed the soldier. "I couldn't imagine not doing it."

"What about you," he asked the next man.

"I am terrified every time I do it, sir," he answered. "I can't say that I like it."

"Why do you do it then?" enquired the General.

"Because I love being with the guys who enjoy doing it," was the reply.

Enthusiasm is like a fire that warms others around you!

The Secret of Yoga

I read about a yogi many years ago. He was the only son of a rich businessman. His father, a rich merchant, suddenly passed away and the son said to himself: "My father has moved on, leaving all his wealth behind – this wealth was of no use to him. He could not carry one single *paisa* with himself. Of what use will all this wealth be to me?" And so he distributes all his wealth to the poor and retires to the solitude of the Himalayan heights. There he goes and spends his life in meditation. He meditates from more to more. He sinks deeper and deeper within himself, until one blessed day in the lotus of the heart within, he beholds the shining Face of God. He meets God face-to-face. And then as he opens his eyes, he finds the one Face of God, the one Divine Face in everything, in everyone around him. God in the mountains, God in the stone, God in the tree, God in the shrub, God in the plant, God in the animal,

God in every man, God in every grain of sand, God in every drop of water, God in every ray of sunshine. And he begins to exclaim:

Jidhar dekhta hun udhar Tu hi Tu hai!
Ke har shai mein jalwa Tera hubahu hai!
Wherever I turn, I behold Thee, Lord!
In every thing I see, I perceive Thy splendour.

This is the experience of every true yogi.

And now he descends from the mountain heights. He comes to the plains below. He goes to the villages, where dwell the poor and needy ones. He carries with himself medicinal herbs. He moves on from one cottage to another, distributing medicinal herbs to the poor and the sick. He meets them in love. He speaks to them. He looks into their needs. He shows them the right way to true happiness, true *ananda*. And every day in the morning and in the evening he goes and sits underneath a tree to meditate.

One day as he is sitting under the tree in meditation, the King of Banaras, proud of his power, intoxicated with drink, happens to pass by. The king sees this yogi sitting underneath a tree. He comes near the yogi and says to him: "O, you who sit with closed eyes, tell me what is it that you teach?"

The yogi does not open his eyes, and the king feels offended. He unsheathes his sword and holding it in his hands says: "If you will not open your eyes, if you will not give me an answer, I shall kill you."

Then it is that the yogi opens his eyes. And looking quietly, gently, lovingly into the face of the king, he says: "O king, you cannot kill me, for I am deathless. I am immortal. I am immutable. I am eternal. You can but destroy this body."

The king is amazed at the fearlessness of this yogi. And he feels ashamed of his conduct. He looks into the eyes of the yogi and finds that they are lit up with a strange, mystic light. He falls down at the feet of the yogi and begs for forgiveness. And he says to the yogi: "O yogi, do kindly tell me, what is it that you teach?" And the yogi says to him: "O king, this is what I teach. Cleanse your heart. Be humble. And give the service of love to all who suffer and are in pain."

In these few simple words is given to us the very essence of the message of yoga. In these few simple words is given to us the very secret of the life of yoga: "Cleanse your heart, be humble and give the service of love to those who suffer and are in pain."

Empty Hands

The name Mahmoud of Gazni, once spelt terror all over India. Wherever he went, he looted, pillaged, kidnapped and killed. In those days, the temples of this country were repositories of great riches. The idols were built with precious metals, and adorned with precious gems. Mahmoud of Gazni ransacked these temples, killed the priests and the gurus and looted the wealth from the temples. He was so rich that he had huge vaults built to store all the gold and silver and precious stones that he had looted.

All the wealth that he had amassed was of no avail to this ruthless conqueror, when death came to him – as it must, to all of us. He lay on his death-bed in profound agony, tortured by the memory of his multiple crimes and sins. He had lived a life tainted by greed, lust and violence. All the wealth which he had captured could not bring him a moment's peace in those crucial final hours of his earthly life. In desperation, he asked to be taken to his harem, so that he could look at the women whom he had enslaved – but they turned their faces away from him, for he had abducted and kidnapped them and outraged their modesty. He asked to be carried to his treasure-house, but the gems and gold he had collected brought no relief to his anguished soul. At last, he called his ministers and counsellors, and warned them not to live as he had lived.

He instructed them thus: "When I die, open my hands and let them hang loose outside my coffin as you take my body in a funeral procession all over the region. Let the people realise that despite all the wealth I looted, I had to leave this world empty handed."

Running Straight

There were three boys who were loafing on the street, fighting with each other. A man happened to pass by and he said to them, "Come boys, and stop fighting. I want you to run a race and I shall give the winner a prize!"

When they heard this, the boys gathered around him, eager to start the race. But his instructions were unusual. He said to them, "I shall stand there at a distance, and you must reach me. But the winner is not the one who runs the fastest but the one who runs the straightest! I will give the signal for you to start, and you must take off and run straight to me."

So the man went up to a distant point and gave the signal: "Ready! Get set! Go!"

The boys ran. The first boy kept looking at his feet to make sure he was running straight. The second one kept looking to his right and left to align himself. But the third one did not look here or there. His eyes were on the man who stood at a distance and he ran straight to reach him. The third boy was the winner – the one who ran straightest. How did he do it? He had his eyes fixed on his goal!

My Father Is Holding the Rope

A botanist, who was collecting samples from a hill slope came across some rare species of flowers, which were located in a narrow ravine, just beneath a steep precipice. He was very anxious to collect a few specimens. But how could he reach the flowers?

He thought for a while. Then he called his eight-year-old son, who was out for the day with him. He tied a rope around the boy's waist. He explained to the little boy what he had to do and which samples he had to collect. Then he gently lowered the boy down the edge of the cliff.

When the boy was drawn up after having successfully accomplished his errand, someone asked him, "Tell me, little one, weren't you afraid?"

"No, of course not!" answered the boy. "My father was holding the rope!"

If only we could develop such faith then we could sail smoothly even during the stormiest weather!

Bald Before His Time!

Have you heard the story of the man who had two wives? One was old – nearer to him in age, while the second was much younger. The younger one wanted her husband to appear young. So, whenever she saw a grey hair on his head, she would pull it out, day after day.

The first wife, on the other hand, was anxious that *she* should not appear to be older than her husband. And so, she took to the habit of pulling out some of his black hair, day after day. She was convinced that this would make him appear mature and respectable.

The result? The man soon lost all the hair on his head, becoming bald before he was fifty years of age!

You Need a Ladder!

Have you heard the name of Jesse Owen? He was the black American athlete who won three Olympic gold medals and created a record at the Munich games. Jesse was born with scrawny legs –

they were lean, weak and bony. But one day, the man who was known as the fastest runner in the world, Charlie Paddock, came to his school. Addressing the boys, Paddock said, "You can be what you want to be in life. Decide what you want to be, then go to God and ask Him to help you become what you want to be."

These words penetrated young Jesse's consciousness. After the lecture, he went up on the dais to meet Charlie Paddock and said to him, "Will you shake hands with me?" Paddock smiled and shook hands with him and Jesse felt as if an electric current passed through his entire body. He went out to the playground and started jumping. He kept on jumping, and in this upbeat mood, he met the sports coach and said to him, "I have a dream! I have a dream!" The coach asked him, "My boy, what is your dream?" Jesse Owen, the boy with the scrawny legs, replied, "I want to be the fastest man alive – like Charlie Paddock!"

The coach patted the boy on the shoulder and said to him, "It is good to have a dream, but you must build a ladder to reach the dream!"

What is the ladder that one must build to reach one's dream? This ladder is made up of four rungs – the four rungs are determination, dedication, discipline and a positive attitude.

Jesse Owen built this ladder, and the dream he cherished came true one day. Jesse entered the Olympic Games. He ran the 100 metres and won gold; he ran 400 metres and won gold; as for high jump, he not only won gold, but created an Olympic record that remained unbeaten for several years to come!

Just imagine – a weak boy with scrawny legs set a goal for himself, and achieved it! And yet we complain, "I don't have the strength … I don't have the resources … I don't have the influence to achieve what I want!"

Association With a Saint

Narada, the sage whose life was devoted to his Lord Narayana, was on one of his pilgrimages. One night, he received the hospitality of a poor, childless couple, who served him with deep love and piety. In the morning, when Narada was about to depart, the householder humbly begged him, "You are beloved of Lord Vishnu. O please tell Him to bless us with a child."

Narada was so moved by the request that he made a beeline to Vaikunth, where he met Lord Vishnu. "Dear Lord, be merciful to this humble devotee of yours. Bless that man with a child," implored the sage.

"I am sorry," said the Lord. "It is not in the destiny of that man to have a child."

Narada went on his way, disappointed.

Five years later, happening to pass the same way, he was once again received by the hospitable couple.

To his amazement, he saw not one, but two children playing at the door of the hut.

"Whose children are these?" he asked in disbelief.

"Ours," said the man. "Soon after you left us last time, our prayers were answered. My wife and I have been truly blessed."

Narada hastened to confront Lord Vishnu. "How could you be so mistaken?" he shouted. "You said it was not in the destiny of that man to have children! Now he has two of them!"

The Lord laughed aloud. "That must be the doing of a saint," he said. "Surely you know Narada, association with a saint has the power to change destiny!"

More than Human

A famous and successful surgeon once invited a friend to watch a complex surgery that he was about to perform. As the surgeon went through the laborious process of preparing himself for the operation, the friend was surprised to see that he seemed a little tense.

"All set?" the friend asked him gently.

"Almost," replied the surgeon, and then stopped what he was doing and bowed his head for a moment. Then, calm and relaxed, he led the way to the Operation Theatre.

During the surgery, his hand never faltered; his concentration never wavered. The complicated procedure was accomplished smoothly and successfully.

Later, the friend said to him, "I was surprised that you prayed before you started. I thought that a surgeon only relied on his own ability."

He answered, "A surgeon is only human. He can't work miracles by himself. I am certain that science could not have advanced as far as it has, were it not for something more than man. You see," he concluded, "I feel so close to God when I am operating, that I do not know where my skill ends, and His begins."

Let us learn to rely more and more on God, if we wish to succeed. God invites us to hand our problems over to Him. Do you have a better option than the best?

The *Baniya* and the Sepoy

A holy man, in his youth, had served in the army – that is, long before he renounced the world and took to the life of the spirit.

At that time, he had been posted in Rawalpindi. The British Government of the day had sent his platoon to Kabul to quell a Pathan uprising which was proving to be a threat to the local British authorities. One of the members of the contingent was an Indian sepoy, who met with a terrible fate. The mare that he was riding was a wild beast; getting out of control, it galloped away with its rider right into the camp of the Pathans. The fierce Pathan insurgents ruthlessly shot down both horse and rider.

The tragic news of the soldier's demise was conveyed to his family in India. His next-of-kin arrived to settle his accounts and take away all his belongings. The Army authorities paid up all the money and allowances that were due to him.

The dead soldier had entrusted a sum of two thousand rupees with the local *baniya* – the Army grocer. This was probably the custom among the sepoys at that time – whenever they were able to save some money, they would deposit it with the *baniya* for safe-keeping. The *baniya* decided that he would not mention this fact to the dead soldier's relatives. It was indeed, an evil temptation to defraud a dead man – the grocer yielded to it, and pocketed the money quietly. The dead man's relatives returned home, and the *baniya* was very pleased with himself.

Twenty years later, the holy man was brought face to face with the *baniya,* once again. Times had changed! India was now free. Pakistan and Afghanistan were independent nations. As I said, the holy man had left the army and acquired *sanyas.* Accompanied by a few of his disciples, he had gone to the holy city of Haridwar to take a dip in the sacred Ganga. On the return trip, they halted at a town called Saharanpur. It was here that they met the *baniya* from Rawalpindi.

"Don't you remember me, Swamiji?" he asked eagerly. "I am the same *baniya* who used to supply rations to your platoon in Rawalpindi. I have settled down here in this town after partition. I entreat you, Swamiji, to bless my home with your visit. You and your disciples must come and spend the night in my house. I won't take no for an answer. Please do come, Swamiji, I beg of you!"

They could not turn down his persistent invitation, and so accompanied him to his house. He treated them with great courtesy and hospitality. An elaborate feast was prepared for them, and they were requested to partake of the food set before them.

As they sat down to eat, they heard the weeping and wailing of a woman from within the house.

"What's that?" enquired the holy man, startled. "It sounds like someone is in great anguish. Is any of your family members ill?"

"Never mind that, Swamiji," said the *baniya* hastily. "It is … it's nothing. I beg you to begin your dinner, for it is very late already."

The sobbing was so persistent that the guests were deeply disturbed. "Dinner can wait, my friend," the holy man said to the *baniya*. "Please attend to the lady – whoever she may be. She seems to be in great distress."

"I shall attend to her by and by, Swamiji," said the *baniya*. "But I beg you to partake of dinner and bless this home."

"My friend, we are not so heartless that we can eat in peace while someone in the house is evidently in pain and grief," the holy man said firmly. "Tell me who is crying, and why she is crying."

"What can I say *maharaj*," said the *baniya*, who was barely able to control his tears now. "My twenty year old son passed away just two days ago, and his young widow is weeping and mourning for him. She is barely seventeen years old. What can she do but cry?"

His guests were horrified to hear this. "It's not even two days since your son passed away!" they exclaimed. "What on earth possessed you to invite us home at such a time? How can you offer us a banquet when your family is in mourning?"

"I have done it with good reason," sighed the *baniya*. "If you want to know the truth, here it is." And he began to narrate his painful story.

"Twenty five years ago, when my contract with the army expired, I returned home. I set up a shop, and sometime later, I was married. Soon, we had a son. I brought him up well; nothing that he wanted was ever denied to him. When he was grown up, I found a beautiful bride for him, and they were happily married.

"All of a sudden, my son was struck by a strange illness. I spared no expenses to give him the best possible treatment. But the doctors could not cure him. I have lost count of the eminent physicians I consulted; but all their medicines were of no avail. He grew from bad to worse.

"One day, a friend told me of a *maulvi*, who was highly regarded by everyone. He suggested that I should bring the *maulvi* home for my son's treatment. I promptly brought him home, and he recited a few prayers and incantations for my son.

"When the recital was over, I realised that I had just two and a half rupees with me at home. I offered it to the *maulvi* and explained it was all I had at that time. I requested him to accept it with grace, and told him I would pay him later.

"As I pressed the money into the *maulvi's* hand, my son laughed out aloud! The *maulvi* was very happy. 'My prayers have had a very beneficial effect on the patient already,' he declared. 'I am confident that he will be up and about very soon.'

"When the *maulvi* had left, I went to my son's bedside and asked him why he had laughed. 'Are you feeling better now?' I enquired anxiously.

'Yes father, I am feeling much better,' he said. 'I am at peace now, for you have settled my account.'

'What account, son?' I asked him, bewildered.

'Father, I want you to know the truth now,' he said. 'I am the Indian sepoy who was killed in Kabul, whose money you did not return to his family. I was reborn as your son, so that you could settle my old debt. The two and a half rupees you just paid to the *maulvi* has finally settled our old account. The purpose of this life of mine has now been fulfilled, and so I laughed out loud. Now, my time with you is over. I have received from you every *paisa* that was due to me, and I shall depart from this earth now.'

'You cannot leave us!' I cried in despair. 'Why, you are just married, and your young bride lives in the hope that you will soon be better, and you two will lead a happy life together!'

'My new bride is none other than the wild mare which wilfully carried me into the enemy camp, and brought about our death,' my son replied. 'It is to pay for this that she will now have to spend the rest of her life as a widow, mourning and lamenting my loss!'"

Such is the Law of Karma! It is a Universal Law. It is a scientific law: As you sow, so shall you reap! We cannot sow thistles and reap mangoes.

Let us be careful of what we are sowing!

God Is!

A famous artist in Mexico had painted a beautiful landscape. It was displayed for public viewing at a five-star hotel. People poured in to admire the masterpiece – a brilliant reproduction of green, rolling countryside, beautiful flowers, blue skies and distant forests.

Across the top of the canvas were written the following words in bold letters: GOD DOES NOT EXIST.

Thousands of admiring visitors moved past the painting every day. Many of them were shocked or upset by the message of denial, but they certainly did not show it. How strange and incompatible with the picture it seemed!

One day, a large group of young men arrived at the hotel. They entered the gallery where the painting was displayed and quietly set to work with paint cans and brushes they had brought along with them. No one could see what they were up to. Were they vandals who would destroy the masterpiece? Would they alter the painting or deface it?

The young men finished what they were doing and left as quickly as they had entered. Crowds surged into the gallery to see what change they had effected.

At first, no one could see any visible difference in the masterpiece. But careful scrutiny revealed that the words of denial had been brushed out completely. Only one word remained in triumphant affirmation: GOD.

What we need above all else today is the rediscovery of the great truth that God *is* – that He is real; that we need to renew our faith in Him.

We Are Responsible for What Happens to Us

What we do unto others will inevitably, in the near or remote future, return to us in one form or another. This is an inviolable, inescapable law of life. If we perpetrate evil, violence or cruelty, these will invariably find their way back to us.

The striking illustration of this law is the story of King Dhritarashtra in the Mahabharata. At the end of the Kurukshetra war, Sri Krishna comes to meet the Pandavas, who are now responsible for their aged, blind uncle, King Dhritarashtra, for all his hundred sons, the Kauravas, have perished in the war.

"It is time that I returned to Dwarka now," Sri Krishna tells the sad, depleted family. "Tell me if there is anything I can do for anyone of you before I leave."

The blind, ageing monarch tells him, "Dear Lord! I have done no harm to anyone in my life. I have tried my best to be fair to everyone. Why, oh, why, is it that I have been cursed with such a miserable fate? Not only has God deprived me of eyesight, but I have also lost the comfort of the support of my sons in old age. Each and every one of my hundred brave sons has perished on the battlefield! Why has God been so cruel to me?"

"O King," Sri Krishna says to him, "Look deep within yourself. Enter into your deepest consciousness, where you will find the answer to your own question."

Dhritarashtra does as he is told. He enters into deep meditation, thereby gaining access to the astral self, wherein lies a record of his previous births. He realises that several lives earlier, during one of his many human births, he had been a cruel and proud king. As he goes out riding with his courtiers, he sees a magnificent swan surrounded by its offsprings – a hundred, beautiful signets. In a ruthless and wanton act of cruelty, the tyrant king orders his soldiers to blind the swan and kill all its hundred offsprings …

King Dhritarashtra's question is answered. It is now clear to him that his blindness and the death of his hundred brave sons during this life, are solely due to what he had done once in the remote past.

There was a time in this ancient land of ours, when everyone was fully aware of this great and inscrutable law. Being so aware, people considered the consequences of their actions, and acted with caution and discrimination. Today, alas, we live in oblivion of this Universal Law! If only we would remember this great truth and act according to its precepts, we would surely evolve into a new and noble nation, worthy of our great tradition.

Live and Let Live

There are some people who are so overcome by negative emotions, that they even make their prayer an expression of their hatred and ill will. Such wishes are not really prayers – and even if we address such wishes to God, they are not heeded.

There was a woman, who hated her sister-in-law. The latter decided to travel from India to the US by air. And this woman, who was consumed by hatred, prayed thus to God: "O Lord, listen to my prayer. Let this plane crash, and let my sister-in-law die in the crash."

Such prayers are not even heard by the Divine Lord.

It is said that Madam Chiang Kai Sheik's mother was a devout and pious woman who spent several hours in prayer every day. When Japan made an unexpected aggression on China, Madam Chiang Kai

Sheik was so incensed that she said to her mother, "Mamma, please pray that an earthquake may strike Japan, that Japan may be drowned and lost in the ocean!"

The pious mother said to her, "My child, how can I offer such a prayer? How will God ever accept such a prayer?"

Sydney Walker was a famous lightweight champion boxer. Born in a poor, illiterate family, he had worked as a shoeshine boy before he rose to fame in the boxing ring. It was known to all that Sydney Walker always prayed before he went out to fight. One day, they asked him, "Is it true that you pray every time before you fight? If it is so, what is it that you ask for in your prayer?"

"My prayer is a simple one," answered Sydney Walker. "All I say to God is – God, let this be a good, clean fight. Let no one get hurt in this fight."

That was indeed a prayer motivated by positive, healthy emotions.

The Greatest Honour

There is a story told us concerning Abdullah, a devout Muslim who had gone to worship at the Holy City of Mecca. One night, he was sleeping in a corner of a mosque when he was awakened by the sounds of a conversation. He looked about him and saw that there were two angels who held a list in their hand.

"This then is the List of the Blessed," said one angel.

"Whose name is the first on the list?" enquired the second angel.

"It is Mahbub of Sikander City," replied the first. "He is truly blessed – even though he has never come on pilgrimage to the Holy City."

Hearing this, Abdullah was amazed. How could someone who had not gone on pilgrimage to Mecca be first among the Blessed? To find out more about this man, Abdullah travelled to Sikander City. After a lot of effort and enquiry, he found the man, Mahbub, who turned out to be a cobbler, working in a poor locality, mending people's shoes.

The man was obviously poor and famished. His clothes were tattered and torn. The few coppers he earned hardly sufficed to feed him and his family.

Abdullah spoke to him and found out his story. Over the years, he had struggled to save a few coppers. One day, when he had just managed to put together a little money, he spent every penny he had to buy a special delicacy for his young wife to eat. As he was carrying the precious dish home, he heard the cry of a starving beggar, desperate for food. Profoundly moved by the man's plight, Mahbub placed the dish before him and sat by his side, as the poor man ate. He was thrilled to see the look of joy on the beggar's face, as he ate the delicious dish.

"I have never known such joy in my life," Mahbub concluded.

It was this act of loving service that had given him the place of honour in the register of the Blessed. Other men who had spent vast sums to undertake the holy pilgrimage could not attain this honour – but this poor man who served without any fuss and fanfare was noticed by the angels and given the honour that he so richly deserved!

Not *Work!*

Rodney Smith was a hospice worker, who visited a social service centre in Kolkata. The facilities at the centre were minimal – just long rows of wooden benches with dying people, side by side. But the patients were bathed and wearing clean clothes; and compassionate, caring volunteers and nuns were moving among them. One of the volunteers was mopping up vomit from the floor. When she had finished her work, Mr. Smith asked to speak to her.

"Tell me sister," he said to her. "What is it that sustains you through your work?"

"What work?" asked the sister, smiling.

Rodney Smith was taken aback. She had been cleaning up vomit — and she was asking, "What work?" Suddenly, he noticed the expression in her eyes. They were so clear and radiant. He thought to himself: "She is alive!"

The volunteer smiled at him and asked him, "When you change the diapers of your child, is that *work*?"

Six Eggs for a Good Cause

Booker T. Washington was trying to raise money to buy land for his Institute, which was meant to promote education among underprivileged blacks. One day, an old black woman hobbled into his room, leaning on a stick. "Mr. Washington, God knows the better part of my life has been spent in slavery," she said. "God knows I'm poor and ignorant. But I know you are trying to make life better for black people. I know you are trying to give them education, so that they can make something of their life. I have brought you what I have – six eggs. I want you to put these six eggs into the education of those boys and girls!"

Booker T. Washington said later, "I have received so many gifts and donations for my institution – but nothing touched me so deeply as the sacrificial gift of that noble woman!"

No Short Cuts

A wealthy businessman was about to enrol his son in a famous university. But he was taken aback when he realised that it would be four years before the boy would be granted his basic degree; and in between, there would be eight semesters with midterm tests, assignments and exams at the end of each year.

Frowning, he flipped through the catalogue of courses and demanded of the Dean, "Why does my son have to go through so many courses? Can't you make the whole thing shorter? I want him to get out of it quickly!"

"Certainly, he can take a shorter course," replied the Dean politely. "It all depends on what he wants to make of himself. You see, it takes 20-30 years for an oak tree to grow; but a mushroom springs up overnight."

We are all attracted by short cuts, quick fixes and easy solutions. But, like the oak tree, the mind and character take time to shape up and grow. And we require all eternity to attain to perfection!

Serve Silently!

I remember, one day we were in a garden, sitting at the Lotus Feet of Sadhu Vaswani, when he pointed to some beautiful flowers and said to us, "Look at these flowers! How beautifully they bloom! But they do it silently. Even so must you serve silently."

"These flowers spread their fragrance in silence. Even so must you serve in silence."

Then pointing to the sun, he said, "The sun, even as it shines, sends life-giving warmth and light to the earth. But it shines silently! And remember, there are millions, billions, perhaps trillions upon trillions of creatures whose very existence depends upon the sun, but the sun shines silently. Even so must you serve silently!"

It was Abraham Lincoln who said, "When I am gone, may it be said about me that here was a man who plucked out a thistle wherever a flower could be planted." What a ideal thought, for all of us to follow! Let us go about silently plucking thistles, and planting flowers in their place. When we serve in silence, our work is truly blessed and it will abide in the hearts of many!

There's a Fine to be Paid

La Guardia was a famous and distinguished statesman. He was a former mayor of New York. Many of you may know that an airport of New Jersey is named after him.

Once, he was presiding over a police court, when a trembling, old man was brought before him. His offence was that he had stolen a loaf of bread, as his family was starving.

La Guardia heard the policeman state the case. Then he turned to the old man. "I have to punish you," he told the old man. "The law has to take its course, and it makes no exceptions. I have to sentence you to a fine of ten dollars!"

Ten dollars! The old man was dumbfounded. He did not even possess ten cents!

Impassive as ever, La Guardia continued, "As the ten dollars is to be paid immediately, I give you the amount myself." Reaching into his pocket, he withdrew a ten-dollar bill, which he dropped into the collection box. "And now I remit the fine."

Turning to the large audience who were staring at him with gaping mouths, he continued, "Furthermore, I am going to fine everybody in this courtroom fifty cents, for living in a town where a man had to steal bread in order to eat."

With those words, he ordered his bailiff to collect the fine of fifty cents from each and every one of the onlookers. A hat was passed round and the sum collected was $47.50, which was handed over to the old man, who left the court – free and happy!

He Cared for People

You may have heard of Dunlop tyres! They were manufactured by George C. Dunlop. As a young man, Dunlop was far from wealthy. But he genuinely cared for his old mother, who was an invalid. She was confined to a wheel chair, and George would often propel the chair for her. He found she suffered severe jolting and discomfort, when the steel rims of the wheel chair moved on rough terrain. He wanted to do something that would reduce her discomfort.

In those days, a new material was discovered, which was much talked about. People were beginning to marvel over its flexibility and softness. It was rubber! Dunlop took strands of rubber and wound them around the steel rims of the wheel chair and found that this smoothened considerably, the movements of the wheel, giving a great deal of comfort to his invalid mother. Thus, began the story of Dunlop tyres – first designed to bring comfort to an invalid's life, they made George Dunlop a wealthy man many times over!

Because I Love You ...

As a young nun, Mother Teresa was filled with a burning desire to be around the destitute, homeless and the ailing, and devote her life to their service. However, her superiors at the Convent were concerned about her youth and inexperience and assigned her the task of teaching at a school in India.

Finally, when she was thirty-nine years old, Mother Teresa was permitted to begin the mission of her life in Kolkata. On her very first day, she encountered a dying man lying in a gutter. His body was covered with sores, and a haze of insects swarmed over him. Everyone skirted the corner where he lay, too fussy even to walk near him. Mother Teresa knelt beside him and began to clean his worm-infested sores.

He opened his eyes in shock and disbelief. "Why are you helping me?" he asked her.

She smiled and replied, "Because I love you!"

Is Not the Thief Your Brother?

A thief entered the compound of the Mira School building and broke some water-pipes. The thief was about to carry away the pipes when he was caught by the night watchman and handed over to the police.

Sadhu Vaswani learnt of it the next day and felt sad. He said, "He, whom you call a thief – is he not your brother? Can you disown him? Don't you see your face in his face?"

Sadhu Vaswani sent word to the trying Magistrate, requesting him that he might be pleased to pardon the thief. Before Sadhu Vaswani's message reached the Magistrate, the thief had already pleaded guilty. The Magistrate found himself in a predicament. But he said, "How can I disregard the words of a saint of God?" And the thief was let off!

He ran to Sadhu Vaswani and fell at his feet. The light of repentance shone in his eyes. "I am a poor man," he said to Sadhu Vaswani. "My children are starving. In vain I sought for work to earn an honest rupee. In utter desperation I broke into your compound, little knowing that therein dwelt a saint of God. Please forgive me! Forgive me!"

There were tears in the eyes of the thief. Sadhu Vaswani's eyes also glistened with tears. He embraced the thief, gave him a pair of new clothes and a few rupees, and asked a brother to get him some work.

On another occasion, Sadhu Vaswani said, "Even a harlot is not alien to us. Have faith in her and you will save her!"

Persistence Pays!

You have no doubt heard the name of Daniel Webster – who gave his name to the well-known dictionary. Do you know how long it took him to prepare the very first edition of the dictionary named after him? Thirty-six years! For thirty-six long years, he laboured, he toiled ceaselessly. He could have given up after five years, or ten years or fifteen years. But he did not give up.

It took Gibbon twenty-six years to write that memorable book, *The Decline and Fall of the Roman Empire* – twenty-six painstaking years! Gibbon did not give up his labour of love until it was accomplished.

Ernest Hemingway was awarded the Nobel Prize for literature for his masterpiece, *The Old Man and the Sea.* He revised the manuscript over and over again, before he was satisfied with it and then handed it over to the publisher. We are told that he went over the manuscript 80 times!

All the great ones of humanity who have achieved success in life are the ones who have never, never given up!

Leave It to God!

I remember one of the earliest prayers I offered to God asking for something specific, was when I was in the eighth standard. One of my classmates decided to join the Merchant Navy ship *S. S. Duffrin*, and receive training on it. I was fascinated by the idea, for the sea has always been my first love. The very thought that I would be in the midst of the ocean all the time, that I would be able to see the rolling waves of the sea by the day, and the shining silvery waters by the moonlit night, thrilled me and excited me. I decided that I too, would join the *S. S. Duffrin*.

At what I judged to be an opportune moment, I spoke of it to my revered mother. Much to my disappointment, she would not hear of it. "*Duffrin* is for duffers," she said firmly, for that was the common perception then. Only boys who could not pass their examinations went for training in the Merchant Navy, in those days.

So my mother said to me, "You are not a duffer, you are an intelligent boy. I will not permit you to leave school and join the *S. S. Duffrin*, or any other ship."

I prayed and prayed and prayed. I even fasted for a few days. My prayers were not answered. Today, I am truly grateful that God did not hear my prayers.

As Sadhu Vaswani says, God upsets our plans to set up His own!

Do Your Duty!

Do your duty. When you perform your duty consciously and with full responsibility, your inner instrument *(antahkarna)* is purified.

Do your duty – but develop the spirit of detachment. Attend to your duty in the full awareness that nothing, or no one, belongs to you. You are only an actor – and also a spectator – in the ever unfolding, cosmic drama of life.

You must play this double role as actor and spectator.

Once, a young woman complained to me, "My mother-in-law makes my life miserable. No matter how hard I try, I cannot please her. She treats me so badly that I am desperate. What shall I do?"

"You must treat her well," I said to her. "Show love and mercy to her."

"But she is wicked and cruel," the woman protested.

"She is acting as per her past *karma*," I replied. "I suggest that you sow the seeds of good *karma* by treating her well. Do your duty by her, irrespective of how she treats you. This way, you will ensure the security of your own future."

Do your duty. This is not the rule for the individual alone; it applies to all – to the whole society, to the nation, to the world at large. Kings and Emperors who failed to realise this, were reduced to naught – for they failed to do their regal, political duty as they ought to have done.

The Answer to His Prayer

There was a little boy who devoutly believed in the power of prayer. He prayed constantly and regularly. When there was anything he wanted badly, he would pray, again and again.

One day, he was walking about on the terrace of his house when suddenly his foot slipped. He fell down, sliding rapidly down the sloping roof. Instinctively, he prayed to God, "God! Please save me! Hold me! Don't let me fall to my death. Save me! Hold me!" He had barely ended his prayer when his foot caught on a protruding nail and his fall was arrested. He came to a standstill and said, "God, don't trouble Yourself. There was a nail on the roof and it has saved me from falling."

Foolish as he was, he did not realise that the nail was but an answer to his prayer. But he failed to recognise the answer.

The Influence of Television

This is a true incident that was reported in the US a few years ago.

The local office in a small town found a 3-year-old child standing all alone near a supermarket in the town-centre. She was indeed a little charmer – big, bright eyes, cute pigtails and a penetrating gaze. She was contentedly sucking on her lollipop when a policeman found her. But she would not answer his gentle questions – who she was or where she lived.

He bought her an ice cream and continued his gentle probing. She was enjoying her ice cream now. She looked soulfully at him but refused to open her mouth to divulge any information about herself.

The policeman kept talking to her in baby language and began to go through her pockets, hoping to find some clue to her identity.

Then the little girl spoke for the first time.

"Don't bother," she said in a clear, ringing tone, "I don't carry a gun."

Bemused, the policeman burst out laughing.

Do we ever stop to think what influences and ideas our children are absorbing while they sit glued to the TV – the 'idiot box' as it is called? A child's mind is like plastic – it is so impressionable that it can be conditioned very easily. Therefore, I urge parents to beware and give children *their* company, rather than leave them to the company of the television!

You've Got to *Give* to Get!

A farmer was replacing the fence posts on his farm. As he removed the old ones, he laid them in a pile and began to burn them.

A neighbour who was passing by, stopped to ask him what he was burning and why. "It's those old, useless fence posts of mine that have become weather-beaten now," he replied. "You can see I'm replacing them with these bright, white new posts. I'm burning the old ones because I don't need them anymore."

"In that case," the neighbour ventured, "can I have a couple of them to burn in my fireplace?"

The farmer frowned and said, "No, definitely not," and added sternly, "I sell firewood, you know. I will be glad to deliver it to you on a cash basis."

The fence posts continued to burn, and the neighbour went away miffed. When he had to order his stock of firewood, he took his business elsewhere.

What the farmer failed to realise was that a gift of a few 'useless fence posts' could have gained him a friend and a prospective customer!

You must be prepared to *give* – if you want to get! This applies to successful businessmen too!

Redefining Success

A young doctor who had set up practice in the city was visited by his old father, who came from the village to see him. "Well, son," he said, "how are you doing?"

"I'm doing very badly," said the discouraged young man. "It's an uphill struggle to set up as a doctor here!"

The father's face fell, but he spoke to his son with courage, patience and hope. Later in the day, he accompanied his son to the free dispensary where the doctor offered his services in the evening. He sat in silence in the waiting room, and watched 25 people who were wretched and ill receive medical attention from his son. When the last man had left, he burst out: "I thought you had told me you were doing badly! Why, you have attended to 25 people in just one sitting!"

"There isn't any money in this," said the young man.

"Money!" exclaimed the old man. "What is money in comparison with being useful to your fellowmen?"

Money is not the 'be all' and 'end all' of life. It has been rightly said that you have not lived a perfect day unless you have served someone who will never be able to repay you.

Duty First

There is a legend of a monk, who once beheld the glorious vision of God in his lonely cell. As he was gazing with rapture at the vision, he heard the bell that summoned him to his daily duty – distributing loaves of bread to all the poor people in the village.

With agony, he tore himself away from the glorious vision to attend to the daily, dull routine of his duty. But when he came back, he was surprised and elated to find that God was still there, waiting for him to come back! God met him with the greeting, "I waited for you, because your duty called you. If you had not answered the call of duty, I would have departed!"

"What is the secret of your success?" someone asked George Washington Carver.

"I pray as if everything depends on God," he said. He paused and then added, "I work as if everything depends on me!"

Hence, we have the saying: Pull and pray!

Stone Soup

Let me narrate to you an old story – a children's folk tale dating back to the sixteenth century. It tells us of a traveller who had set out on an arduous journey. He had walked for hours together, and he was weary and hungry. He reached a small village, and he thought to himself, "Perhaps there is someone in this village who will give me something to eat. I shall eat, rest a while and then proceed on my way."

So he knocked at the door of the first cottage he saw. It was opened by a woman, to whom he said, "I am a weary traveller who has walked a long way. Would you be so kind as to give me something to eat?"

"I am sorry," the woman said to him. "I have nothing to give you."

The traveller knocked at the door of every house

and everywhere, he received the same reply. They had nothing to give him.

Finally, he met a villager, who said to him, "I have some water which I can share with you."

"Thank you!" said the delighted traveller. "We shall make stone soup with your water!"

"Stone soup!" exclaimed the villager. "I would like to see how you make stone soup."

The two men lit a fire. The villager brought a cooking pot into which water was poured. The pot was set over the fire; the water began to boil.

A passing villager stopped to stare curiously. "What are you doing?" he wanted to know.

"We are making stone soup," said the traveller cheerfully. "Would you like to join us?"

"But what I would like to know is how on earth one prepares stone soup!"

The traveller took out a smooth, shining stone from his pocket and showed it to the villagers. "This is a magic stone," he told them. "We shall make our soup with this magic stone." And he dropped the stone into the pot of boiling water.

Word spread across the whole village, that a passing stranger was preparing a magical soup with a stone. It was not long before villagers arrived on the scene, one by one.

"What does stone soup taste like?" asked one of them. "I like my soup with plenty of onions."

"Well," said the traveller. "The soup would certainly taste better with a few onions, but we haven't got any."

"Onions?" said another villager. "Why, I have a few onions at home. I shall bring them along."

Soon, the onions were brought and put into the 'soup'. Then, someone else volunteered, "I have a few carrots which you can add," and the carrots went in. Yet another man remembered that he had some potatoes in the garden. These were promptly dug up, washed and added to the soup. By and by, every other villager had brought something or the other to add to the stone soup. What began as just a pot of boiling water, turned into a delicious and nutritious soup, which all the villagers sat down to share. It was indeed a magical feast, which they had all helped to create. Each and every one of them had contributed something to it – each one had made a difference!

Even God Changed His Mind!

There was a man who lived in a North Mumbai suburb. Every day he had to commute across the island city to get to his place of work. From Dombivili to Nariman Point, it was over two hours by road – and that was just one way! He was exhausted by the long way, the pot-holed roads and the traffic jams which made the journey unpredictable.

One morning, as traffic ground to a halt, he sank his weary head on the steering wheel, crying out, "God, oh God, where are You?"

Such was the yearning in this heart-felt cry that the Lord appeared before him at that very moment and said to him, "Here I am, my child. How can I help you?"

"Dear Lord," said the distraught commuter, "all I ask You for is a four-lane freeway from Dombivili to Nariman Point."

The Lord frowned. "Can't you think of higher matters — matters above such material concerns? Consider, if you will, your journey upon the highway of life…"

"You're right, of course Lord," agreed the man, quite abashed. "I will take back my earlier wish and ask You for something more worthwhile — and something which is quite impossible for me as a mere mortal.

"Please grant me the ability to understand my wife, dear Lord. I cannot fathom her mind or her heart. Please help me to understand why she is so unpredictable — why she gets so mad at me sometimes, and why at other times she is so unbelievably loving and kind."

There was a long and uncomfortable silence.

"All right, all right," sighed God. "How many lanes did you say – four or six?"

Sharing God's Blessings

A man was walking along a dusty road in New England. It was a hot day and he was tired. Suddenly he came upon a water-spring. "If you are thirsty, drink!" said a sign put up nearby. He drank the cool water and felt refreshed. A little further up the road was a comfortable wooden bench under a shady tree, with a sign which said, "If you are weary, rest awhile!" Close by, was a basket of delicious looking apples with a sign, "If you are hungry, help yourself".

The stranger was deeply moved by the unknown benefactor who had shown such care and concern for passers-by. As he walked farther, he came upon a humble cottage, outside which sat an old man, whose face beamed with kindness. "Lord's blessings be upon you!" called out the old man, at the sight of the stranger.

"It is your blessings I have enjoyed as I came up the dusty road," replied the stranger. "What is it that has prompted you to be so kind and generous to perfect strangers?"

"Oh, God has given us trees, shade, water, fruits and so much else in plenty," replied the old man. "All I do is share these blessings with weary travellers. It is the least I can do!"

The weary traveller on that hot, dusty road was Sam Walter Ross. His encounter with the kind old man inspired him to write the famous poem, *'The House by the Side of the Road'*.

I Refuse to Be Negative!

David W. Hartman of Pennsylvania became blind when he was eight years old. However, that did not break his spirits and his aspirations. He had always dreamt of studying medicine; and he persisted with his dream.

In those days, people considered visual disability to be a serious and insurmountable 'handicap'. They had a lot of sympathy to offer – but little else. The medical school in which he applied for admission discouraged David severely. They pointed out to him that no one with visual disability had ever completed a medical course. How then could he manage, especially considering the huge volumes of the medical textbooks that students had to read? He would be better off, surely, choosing a less strenuous course that would not tax him so severely.

Hartman refused to be negative. Courageously, he took on the task of "reading" by having twenty-five medical textbooks audio-recorded for him. At twenty-seven, David W. Hartman became the first blind student to complete medical school.

He refused to be negative. He believed and achieved!

The Power of Kindness

The famous English poet, Wordsworth, relates an incident from his early life, which left a lasting impression on him. As he was wandering through a wood, he came across a weak, old man who was trying desperately to cut at the root of a tree. The task was so far beyond his feeble strength, that he was about to collapse. The poet, a young man, seized his axe and at one blow, severed the tangled root. The old man's gratitude was like an avalanche, as the poet recalled in memorable lines:

The tears into his eyes were brought,
And thanks and praises seemed to run
So fast out of his heart,
I thought he never would be done.

Such is the power of a single act of kindness!

A few men were requested to meet Lord Shaftesbury at the railway station. "How shall we know his Lordship?" they enquired.

The answer they received was significant: "You will see a tall man getting out of the train. He will be helping somebody or the other. That will be Lord Shaftesbury."

Indeed, kindness is the true mark of a great man. It is kindness that makes a difference. You, too, can be kind: and you too, can make a difference!